THE POWER TO CREATE

"A signal testimonial to the creative spirit . . . A brilliantly incisive exploration of the creative 'encounter'—the coming to grips of the healthily committed creative artist or thinker with his socio-cultural background and with his own dangerously Promethean impulses. Dr. May sees true creativity as man's highest and healthiest activity."
—*Publishers Weekly*

"*The Courage to Create* is certain to be widely discussed . . . and demands the attention of every thoughtful reader."
—*The Literary Guild*

"Another in Dr. May's extraordinary, wise and hopeful . . . series of nearly poetic meditations on the future of mankind."
—*The Boston Globe*

THE
COURAGE TO
CREATE

□

ROLLO MAY

BANTAM BOOKS
TORONTO • NEW YORK • LONDON • SYDNEY • AUCKLAND

RL 9, IL age 14 and up

THE COURAGE TO CREATE

*A Bantam Book / published by arrangement with
W. W. Norton & Company, Inc.*

PRINTING HISTORY

Norton edition published August 1975
2nd printing ... October 1975   3rd printing .. November 1975
Bantam edition / December 1976
15 printings through December 1983

"The Nature of Creativity" was first published in Creativity
and Its Cultivation, *Harold H. Anderson, ed. (New York, 1959).*
"Creativity and the Unconscious" was first published in Voices:
The Journal of the American Academy of Psychotherapists.
"Creativity and Encounter" was first published in The Ameri-
can Journal of Psychoanalysis *XXIV/1.*
"The Delphic Oracle as Therapist" was first published in The
Reach of Mind: Essays in Memory of Kurt Goldstein, *Mari-
anne L. Simmel, ed (New York, 1968).*

ISBN 0-553-24222-9

Published simultaneously in the United States and Canada

*Bantam Books are published by Bantam Books, Inc. Its trade-
mark, consisting of the words "Bantam Books" and the portrayal of a rooster, is Registered in U.S. Patent and Trademark
Office and in other countries. Marca Registrada. Bantam
Books, Inc., 666 Fifth Avenue, New York, New York 10103.*

PRINTED IN THE UNITED STATES OF AMERICA

H   24 23 22 21 20 19 18 17 16 15

CONTENTS

PREFACE

◻

ALL MY LIFE I have been haunted by the fascinating questions of creativity. Why does an original idea in science and in art "pop up" from the unconscious at a given moment? What is the relation between talent and the creative act, and between creativity and death? Why does a mime or a dance give us such delight? How did Homer, confronting something as gross as the Trojan War, fashion it into poetry which became a guide for the ethics of the whole Greek civilization?

I have asked these questions not as one who stands on the sidelines, but as one who himself participates in art and science. I ask them out of my own excitement, for example, at watching two of my colors on a paper merge into an unpredictable third color. Is it not the distinguishing characteristic of the human being that in the hot race of evolution he pauses for a moment to paint on the cave walls at Lascaux or Altamira those brown-and-red deer and bison which still fill us with amazed admiration and awe? Suppose the apprehension of beauty is itself a way to truth? Suppose that "elegance"—as the word is used by physicists to describe their discoveries—is a key to ultimate reality? Suppose Joyce is right that the artist creates "the uncreated conscience of the race"?

These chapters are a partial record of my ponderings. They had their birth as lectures given at colleges and universities. I had always hesitated to publish them because they seemed incomplete —the mystery of creation still remained. I then realized that this "unfinished" quality would always remain, and that it is a part of the creative process itself. This realization coincided with the fact that many people who had heard the lectures urged that they be published.

The title was suggested by Paul Tillich's *The Courage to Be*, a debt I am glad to acknowledge. But one cannot *be* in a vacuum. We express our being by creating. Creativity is a necessary sequel to being. Furthermore, the word *courage* in my title refers, beyond the first few pages of the first chapter, to that particular kind of courage essential for the creative act. This is rarely acknowledged in our discussions of creativity and even more rarely written about.

I want to express my gratitude to several friends

who have read all or part of the manuscript and have discussed it with me: Ann Hyde, Magda Denes, and Elinor Roberts.

More than is usually the case, this book was a delight to compile, for it gave me cause to ponder all those quotations over again. I only hope the book gives as much pleasure to the reader as it did to me in the compiling of it.

Rollo May
Holderness, New Hampshire

THE
COURAGE TO
CREATE

ONE

□

THE COURAGE TO
CREATE

WE ARE living at a time when one age is dying and the new age is not yet born. We cannot doubt this as we look about us to see the radical changes in sexual mores, in marriage styles, in family structures, in education, in religion, technology, and almost every other aspect of modern life. And behind it all is the threat of the atom bomb, which recedes into the distance but never disappears. To live with sensitivity in this age of limbo indeed requires courage.

A choice confronts us. Shall we, as we feel our

foundations shaking, withdraw in anxiety and panic? Frightened by the loss of our familiar mooring places, shall we become paralyzed and cover our inaction with apathy? If we do those things, we will have surrendered our chance to participate in the forming of the future. We will have forfeited the distinctive characteristic of human beings—namely, to influence our evolution through our own awareness. We will have capitulated to the blind juggernaut of history and lost the chance to mold the future into a society more equitable and humane.

Or shall we seize the courage necessary to preserve our sensitivity, awareness, and responsibility in the face of radical change? Shall we consciously participate, on however small the scale, in the forming of the new society? I hope our choice will be the latter, for I shall speak on that basis.

We are called upon to do something new, to confront a no man's land, to push into a forest where there are no well-worn paths and from which no one has returned to guide us. This is what the existentialists call the anxiety of nothingness. To live into the future means to leap into the unknown, and this requires a degree of courage for which there is no immediate precedent and which few people realize.

1. WHAT IS COURAGE?

This courage will not be the opposite of despair. We shall often be faced with despair, as indeed every sensitive person has been during the last several decades in this country. Hence Kierkegaard and Nietzsche and Camus and Sartre have proclaimed that courage is not the absence of despair; it is, rather, the capacity to move ahead *in spite of despair*.

Nor is the courage required mere stubbornness —we shall surely have to create with others. But if you do not express your own original ideas, if you do not listen to your own being, you will have betrayed yourself. Also you will have betrayed our community in failing to make your contribution to the whole.

A chief characteristic of this courage is that it requires a centeredness within our own being, without which we would feel ourselves to be a vacuum. The "emptiness" within corresponds to an apathy without; and apathy adds up, in the long run, to cowardice. That is why we must always base our commitment in the center of our own being, or else no commitment will be ultimately authentic.

Courage, furthermore, is not to be confused

with rashness. What masquerades as courage may turn out to be simply a bravado used to compensate for one's unconscious fear and to prove one's machismo, like the "hot" fliers in World War II. The ultimate end of such rashness is getting one's self killed, or at least one's head battered in with a policeman's billy club—both of which are scarcely productive ways of exhibiting courage.

Courage is not a virtue or value among other personal values like love or fidelity. It is the foundation that underlies and gives reality to all other virtues and personal values. Without courage our love pales into mere dependency. Without courage our fidelity becomes conformism.

The word *courage* comes from the same stem as the French word *coeur*, meaning "heart." Thus just as one's heart, by pumping blood to one's arms, legs, and brain enables all the other physical organs to function, so courage makes possible all the psychological virtues. Without courage other values wither away into mere facsimiles of virtue.

In human beings courage is necessary to make *being* and *becoming* possible. An assertion of the self, a commitment, is essential if the self is to have any reality. This is the distinction between human beings and the rest of nature. The acorn becomes an oak by means of automatic growth; no commitment is necessary. The kitten similarly becomes a cat on the basis of instinct. *Nature* and *being* are identical in creatures like them. But a man or women becomes fully human only by his or her choices and his or her commitment to them. People attain worth and dignity by the multitude of decisions they make from day to day. These decisions require courage. This is why Paul Tillich speaks of courage as *ontological*—it is essential to our being.

2. PHYSICAL COURAGE

This is the simplest and most obvious kind of courage. In our culture, physical courage takes its form chiefly from the myths of the frontier. Our prototypes have been the pioneer heroes who took the law into their own hands, who survived because they could draw a gun faster than their opponent, who were, above all things, self-reliant and could endure the inevitable loneliness in homesteading with the nearest neighbor twenty miles away.

But the contradictions in our heritage from this frontier are immediately clear to us. Regardless of the heroism it generated in our forebears, this kind of courage has now not only lost its usefulness, but has degenerated into brutality. When I was a child in a small Midwest town, boys were expected to fistfight. But our mothers represented a different viewpoint, so the boys often got licked at school and then whipped for fighting when they came home. This is scarcely an effective way to build character. As a psychoanalyst, I hear time and again of men who had been sensitive as boys and who could not learn to pound others into submission; consequently, they go through life with the conviction that they are cowards.

America is among the most violent of the so-called civilized nations; our homicide rate is three to ten times higher than that of the nations of Europe. An important cause of this is the influence of that frontier brutality of which we are the heirs.

We need a new kind of physical courage that will neither run rampant in violence nor require our assertion of egocentric power *over* other people. I propose a new form of courage of the body: the use of the body not for the development of musclemen, but for the cultivation of sensitivity. This will mean the development of the capacity to listen with the body. It will be, as Nietzsche remarked, a learning to think with the body. It will be a valuing of the body as the means of empathy with others, as expression of the self as a thing of beauty and as a rich source of pleasure.

Such a view of the body is already emerging in America through the influence of yoga, meditation, Zen Buddhism, and other religious psychologies from the Orient. In these traditions, the body is not condemned, but is valued as a source of justified pride. I propose this for our consideration as the kind of physical courage we will need for the new society toward which we are moving.

3. MORAL COURAGE

A second kind of courage is moral courage. The persons I have known, or have known of, who have great moral courage have generally abhorred violence. Take, for example, Aleksander Solzhenitsyn, the Russian author who stood up alone against the might of the Soviet bureaucracy in protest against the inhuman and cruel treatment of men and women in Russian prison camps. His numerous books, written in the best prose of modern Russia, cry out against the crushing of any person, whether physically, psychologically, or spiritually. His moral courage stands out the more clearly since he is not a liberal, but a Russian nationalist. He became the symbol of a value lost sight of in a confused world—that the innate worth of a human being must be revered solely because of his or her humanity and regardless of his or her politics. A Dostoevskian character out of old Russia (as Stanley Kunitz describes him), Solzhenitsyn proclaimed, "I would gladly give my life if it would advance the cause of truth."

Apprehended by the Soviet police, he was taken to prison. The story is told that he was disrobed and marched out before a firing squad. The purpose of the police was to scare him to death if they could not silence him psychologically; their bullets were blanks. Undaunted, Solzhenitsyn now lives as an exile in Switzerland, where he pursues his gadfly role and levels the same kind of criticism at other nations, like the United States, at the points where our democracy obviously stands in need of radical revision. So long as there exist persons with the moral courage of a Solzhenitsyn, we can be sure that the triumph of "man, the robot" has not yet arrived.

Solzhenitsyn's courage, like that of many persons of similar moral valor, arose not only out of his audaciousness, but also out of his compassion for the human suffering he saw about him during his own sentence in the Soviet prison camp. It is highly significant, and indeed almost a rule, that moral courage has its source in such identification through one's own sensitivity with the suffering of one's fellow human beings. I am tempted to call this "perceptual courage" because it depends on one's capacity to *perceive*, to let one's self see the suffering of other people. If we let ourselves experience the evil, we will be forced to do something about it. It is a truth, recognizable in all of us, that when we don't want to become involved, when we don't want to confront even the *issue* of whether or not we'll come to the aid of someone who is being unjustly treated, we block off our perception, we blind ourselves to the other's suffering, we cut off our empathy with the person needing help. Hence the most prevalent form of cowardice in our day hides behind the statement "I did not want to become involved."

4. SOCIAL COURAGE

The third kind of courage is the opposite to the just described apathy; I call it social courage. It is the courage to relate to other human beings, the capacity to risk one's self in the hope of achieving meaningful intimacy. It is the courage to invest one's self over a period of time in a relationship that will demand an increasing openness.

Intimacy requires courage because risk is inescapable. We cannot know at the outset how the relationship will affect us. Like a chemical mixture, if one of us is changed, both of us will be. Will we grow in self-actualization, or will it destroy us? The one thing we can be certain of is that if we let ourselves fully into the relationship for good or evil, we will not come out unaffected.

A common practice in our day is to avoid working up the courage required for authentic intimacy by shifting the issue to the body, making it a matter of simple physical courage. It is easier in our society to be naked physically than to be naked psychologically or spiritually—easier to share our body than to share our fantasies, hopes, fears, and aspirations, which are felt to be more personal and the sharing of which is experienced as making us more vulnerable. For curious reasons we are shy about sharing the things that matter most. Hence people short-circuit the more "dangerous" building of a relationship by leaping immediately into bed. After all, the body is an object and can be treated mechanically.

But intimacy that begins and remains on the physical level tends to become inauthentic, and we later find ourselves fleeing from the emptiness. Authentic social courage requires intimacy on the many levels of the personality simultaneously. Only by doing this can one overcome personal alienation. No wonder the meeting of new persons brings a throb of anxiety as well as the joy of expectation; and as we go deeper into the relationship each new depth is marked by some new joy and new anxiety. Each meeting can be a harbinger of an unknown fate in store for us but also a stimulus toward the exciting pleasure of authentically knowing another person.

Social courage requires the confronting of two different kinds of fear. These were beautifully described by one of the early psychoanalysts, Otto Rank. The first he calls the "life fear." This is the fear of living autonomously, the fear of being abandoned, the need for dependency on someone else. It shows itself in the need to throw one's self so completely into a relationship that one has no self left with which to relate. One becomes, in effect, a reflection of the person he or she loves— which sooner or later becomes boring to the partner. This is the fear of self-actualization, as Rank described it. Living some forty years before the days of women's liberation, Rank averred that this kind of fear was most typical of women.

The opposite fear Rank called the "death fear." This is the fear of being totally absorbed by the other, the fear of losing one's self and one's autonomy, the fear of having one's independence taken away. This, said Rank, is the fear most associated with men, for they seek to keep the back door open to beat a hasty retreat in case the relationship becomes too intimate.

Actually, if Rank had lived on into our day he would have agreed that both kinds of fear have to be confronted, in varying proportions to be sure, by both men and women. All our lives we oscillate between these two fears. They are, indeed, the forms of anxiety that lie in wait for anyone who cares for another. But the confronting of these two fears, and the awareness that one grows not only by being one's self but also by participating in other selves, is necessary if we are to move toward self-realization.

Albert Camus, in *Exile and the Kingdom,* wrote a story that illustrates these two opposite kinds of courage. "The Artist at Work" is a tale of a poor Parisian painter who could scarcely get enough money to buy bread for his wife and children. When the artist is on his death bed, his best friend finds the canvas on which the painter was working. It is blank except for one word, unclearly written and in very small letters, that appears in the center. The word can either be *solitary*—being alone; keeping one's distance from events, maintaining the peace of mind necessary for listening to one's deeper self. Or it can be *solidary*—"living in the market place"; solidarity, involvement, or identifying with the masses, as Karl Marx put it. Opposites though they are, both solitude and solidarity are essential if the artist is to produce works that are not only significant to his or her age, but that will also speak to future generations.

5. ONE PARADOX OF COURAGE

A curious paradox characteristic of every kind of courage here confronts us. It is the seeming contradiction that *we must be fully committed, but we must also be aware at the same time that we might possibly be wrong*. This dialectic relationship between conviction and doubt is characteristic of the highest types of courage, and gives the lie to the simplistic definitions that identify courage with mere growth.

People who claim to be *absolutely* convinced that their stand is the only right one are dangerous. Such conviction is the essence not only of dogmatism, but of its more destructive cousin, fanaticism. It blocks off the user from learning new truth, and it is a dead giveaway of unconscious doubt. The person then has to double his or her protests in order to quiet not only the opposition but his or her own unconscious doubts as well.

Whenever I heard—as we all did often during the Nixon-Watergate days—the "I am absolutely convinced" tone or the "I want to make this absolutely clear" statement emanating from the White House, I braced myself, for I knew that some dishonesty was being perpetrated by the telltale sign of overemphasis. Shakespeare aptly said, "The lady [or the politician] doth protest too much, methinks." In such a time, one longs for the presence of a leader like Lincoln, who openly admitted his doubts and as openly preserved his commitment. It is infinitely safer to know that the man at the top has his doubts, as you and I have ours, yet has the courage to move ahead in spite of these doubts. In contrast to the fanatic who has stockaded himself against new truth, the person with the courage to believe and at the same time to admit his doubts is flexible and open to new learning.

Paul Cézanne strongly believed that he was discovering and painting a new form of space which would radically influence the future of art, yet he was at the same time filled with painful and ever-present doubts. The relationship between commitment and doubt is by no means an antagonistic one. Commitment is healthiest when it is not *without* doubt, but *in spite of* doubt. To believe fully and at the same moment to have doubts is not at all a contradiction: it presupposes a greater respect for truth, an awareness that truth always goes beyond anything that can be said or done at any given moment. To every thesis there is an antithesis, and to this there is a synthesis. Truth is thus a never-dying process. We then know the meaning of the statement attributed to Leibnitz: "I would walk twenty miles to listen to my worst enemy if I could learn something."

6. CREATIVE COURAGE

This brings us to the most important kind of courage of all. Whereas moral courage is the righting of wrongs, creative courage, in contrast, is the discovering of new forms, new symbols, new patterns on which a new society can be built. Every profession can and does require some creative courage. In our day, technology and engineering, diplomacy, business, and certainly teaching, all of these professions and scores of others are in the midst of radical change and require courageous persons to appreciate and direct this change. The need for creative courage is in direct proportion to the degree of change the profession is undergoing.

But those who present directly and immediately the new forms and symbols are the artists—the dramatists, the musicians, the painters, the dancers, the poets, and those poets of the religious sphere we call saints. They portray the new symbols in the form of images—poetic, aural, plastic, or dramatic, as the case may be. They live out their imaginations. The symbols only dreamt about by most human beings are expressed in graphic form by the artists. But in our appreciation of the created work—let us say a Mozart quintet—we also are performing a creative art. When we engage a painting, which we have to do especially with modern art if we are authentically to see it, we are experiencing some new moment of sensibility. Some new vision is triggered in us by our contact with the painting; something unique is born in us. This is why appreciation of the music or painting or other works of the creative person is also a creative act on our part.

If these symbols are to be understood by us, we must identify with them as we perceive them. In Beckett's play *Waiting for Godot,* there are no intellectual discussions of the failure of communication in our time; the failure is simply *presented* there on the stage. We see it most vividly, for example, when Lucky, who, at his master's order to "Think," can only sputter out a long speech that has all the pomposity of a philosophical discourse but is actually pure gibberish. As we involve ourselves more and more in the drama, we see represented on stage, larger than life, our general human failure to communicate authentically.

We see on the stage, in Beckett's play, the lone, bare tree, symbolic of the lone, bare relationship the two men have as they wait together for a Godot who never appears; and it elicits from us a similar sense of the alienation that we and multitudes of others experience. The fact that most people have no clear awareness of their alienation only makes this condition more powerful.

In Eugene O'Neill's *The Iceman Cometh,* there are no explicit discussions of the disintegration of our society; it is shown as a reality in the drama. The nobility of the human species is not talked *about,* but is presented as a vacuum on the stage. Because this nobility is such a vivid absence, an emptiness that fills the play, you leave the theater with a profound sense of the importance of being human, as you do after having seen *Macbeth* or *King Lear*. O'Neill's capacity to communicate that experience places him among the significant tragedians of history.

Artists can portray these experiences in music or words or clay or marble or on canvas because they express what Jung calls the "collective unconscious." This phrase may not be the most felicitous, but we know that each of us carries in buried dimensions of our being some basic forms, partly generic and partly experiential in origin. It is these the artist expresses.

Thus the artists—in which term I hereafter include the poets, musicians, dramatists, plastic artists, as well as saints—are a "dew" line, to use McLuhan's phrase; they give us a "distant early warning" of what is happening to our culture. In the art of our day we see symbols galore of alienation and anxiety. But at the same time there is form amid discord, beauty amid ugliness, some human love in the midst of hatred—a love that temporarily triumphs over death but always loses out in the long run. The artists thus express the spiritual meaning of their culture. Our problem is: Can we read their meaning aright?

Take Giotto in what is called the "little Renaissance", which burgeoned in the fourteenth century. In contrast to the two-dimensional medieval mosaics, Giotto presents a new way of seeing life and nature: he gives his paintings three dimensions, and we now see human beings and animals expressing and calling forth from us such specific human emotions as care, or pity, or grief, or joy. In the previous, two-dimensional mosaics in the churches of the Middle Ages, we feel no human being is necessary to see them— they have their own relationship to God. But in Giotto, a human being *viewing* the picture is required; and this human being must take his stance as an *individual* in relation to the picture. Thus the new humanism and the new relation to nature that were to become central in the Renaissance are here born, a hundred years *before* the Renaissance proper.

In our endeavor to grasp these symbols of art, we find ourselves in a realm that beggars our usual conscious thinking. Our task is quite beyond the reach of logic. It brings us to an area in which there are many paradoxes. Take the idea expressed in Shakespeare's four lines at the end of Sonnet 64:

> Ruin hath taught me thus to ruminate,
> That time will come and take my love away.
> This thought is as a death, which cannot choose
> But weep to have that which it fears to lose.

If you have been trained to accept the logic of

our society, you will ask: "Why does he have to 'weep to have' his love? Why can he not enjoy his love?" Thus our logic pushes us always toward adjustment—an adjustment to a crazy world and to a crazy life. And worse yet, we cut ourselves off from understanding the profound depths of experience that Shakespeare is here expressing.

We have all had such experiences, but we tend to cover them over. We may look at an autumn tree so beautiful in its brilliant colors that we feel like weeping; or we may hear music so lovely that we are overcome with sadness. The craven thought then creeps into our consciousness that maybe it would have been better not to have seen the tree at all or not to have heard the music. Then we wouldn't be faced with this uncomfortable paradox—knowing that "time will come and take my love away," that everything we love will die. But the essence of being human is that, in the brief moment we exist on this spinning planet, we can love some persons and some things, in spite of the fact that time and death will ultimately claim us all. That we yearn to stretch the brief moment, to postpone our death a year or so is surely understandable. But such postponement is bound to be a frustrating and ultimately a losing battle.

By the creative act, however, we *are* able to reach beyond our own death. This is why creativity is so important and why we need to confront the problem of the relationship between creativity and death.

7

Consider James Joyce, who is often cited as the greatest of modern novelists. At the very end of *A Portrait of the Artist as a Young Man*, he has his young hero write in his diary:

Welcome, O life! I go to encounter for the millionth time the reality of experience and to forge in the smithy of my soul the uncreated conscience of my race.

What a rich and profound statement that is!—"I go to encounter for the millionth time." In other words, every creative encounter is a *new* event; every time requires another assertion of courage. What Kierkegaard said about love is also true of creativity: every person must start at the beginning. And to encounter "the reality of experience" is surely the basis for all creativity. The task will be "to forge in the smithy of my soul," as arduous as the blacksmith's task of bending red-hot iron in his smithy to make something of value for human life.

But note especially the last words, to forge "the uncreated conscience of my race." Joyce is here saying that conscience is not something handed down ready-made from Mount Sinai, despite reports to the contrary. It is created, first of all, out of the inspiration derived from the artist's symbols and forms. Every authentic artist is engaged in this creating of the conscience of the race, even though he or she may be unaware of the fact. The artist is not a moralist by conscious intention, but is concerned only with hearing and expressing the vision within his or her own being. But out of the symbols the artist sees and creates—as Giotto created the forms for the Renaissance—there is later hewn the ethical structure of the society.

Why is creativity so difficult? And why does it require so much courage? Is it not simply a matter of clearing away the dead forms, the defunct symbols and the myths that have become lifeless? No. Joyce's metaphor is much more accurate: it is as difficult as forging in the smithy of one's soul. We are faced with a puzzling riddle indeed.

Some help comes from George Bernard Shaw. Having attended a concert given by the violinist Heifitz, he wrote the following letter when he got home:

My dear Mr. Heifitz,

My wife and I were overwhelmed by your concert. If you continue to play with such beauty, you will certainly die young. No one can play with such perfection without provoking the jealousy of the gods. I earnestly implore you to play something badly every night before going to bed. . . .

Beneath Shaw's humorous words there is, as there often was with him, a profound truth—creativity provokes the jealousy of the gods. This is why authentic creativity takes so much courage: *an active battle with the gods is occurring.*

I cannot give you any complete explanation of why this is so; I can only share my reflections. Down through the ages, authentically creative figures have consistently found themselves in such a struggle. Degas once wrote, "A painter paints a picture with the same feeling as that with which a criminal commits a crime." In Judaism and Christianity the second of the Ten Commandments adjures us, "You shall not make yourself a graven image, or any likeness of anything that is in the heavens above or that is in the earth beneath, or that is in the water under the earth." I am aware that the ostensible purpose of this commandment was to protect the Jewish people from idol worship in those idol-strewn times.

But the commandment also expresses the timeless fear that every society harbors of its artists, poets, and saints. For they are the ones who threaten the status quo, which each society is devoted to protecting. It is clearest in the struggles occurring in Russia to control the utterances of the poets and the styles of the artists; but it is true also in our own country, if not so blatant. Yet in spite of this divine prohibition, and despite the courage necessary to flout it, countless Jews and Christians through the ages have devoted themselves to painting and sculpting and have continued to make graven images and produce symbols in one form or another. Many of them have had the same experience of a battle with the gods.

A host of other riddles, which I can only cite without comment, are bound up with this major one. One is that genius and psychosis are so close to each other. Another is that creativity carries such an inexplicable guilt feeling. A third is that so many artists and poets commit suicide, and often at the very height of their achievement.

As I tried to puzzle out the riddle of the battle with the gods, I went back to the prototypes in human cultural history, to those myths that illuminate how people have understood the creative act. I do not use this term *myth* in the common present-day deteriorated meaning of "falsehood." This is an error that could be committed only by a society that has become so inebriated with adding up empirical facts that it seals off the deeper wisdom of human history. I use *myth* as meaning, rather, a dramatic presentation of the moral wisdom of the race. The myth uses the totality of the senses rather than just the intellect.

In ancient Greek civilization, there is the myth of Prometheus, a Titan living on Mount Olympus, who saw that human beings were without

fire. His stealing fire from the gods and giving it
to humankind is taken henceforth by the Greeks
as the beginning of civilization, not only in cook-
ing and in the weaving of textiles, but in philosophy, science, drama, and in culture itself.

But the important point is that *Zeus was out-*
raged. He decreed that Prometheus be punished
by being bound to Mount Caucasus, where a
vulture was to come each morning and eat away
his liver which would grow again at night. This
element in the myth, incidentally, is a vivid symbol of the creative process. All artists have at
some time had the experience at the end of the
day of feeling tired, spent, and so certain they
can never express their vision that they vow to
forget it and start all over again on something
else the next morning. But during the night their
"liver grows back again." They arise full of energy
and go back with renewed hope to their task,
again to strive in the smithy of their soul.

Least anyone think the myth of Prometheus
can be brushed aside as merely an idiosyncratic
tale concocted by playful Greeks, let me remind
you that in the Judeo-Christian tradition almost
exactly the same truth is presented. I refer to the
myth of Adam and Eve. This is the drama of the
emerging of moral consciousness. As Kierkegaard
said in relation to this myth (and to all myths),
the truth that happens internally is presented as
though it were external. The myth of Adam is

re-enacted in every infant, beginning a few months after birth and developing into recognizable form at the age of two or three, though ideally it should continue enlarging all the rest of one's life. The eating of the apple of the tree of the knowledge of good and evil symbolizes the dawn of human consciousness, moral conscience and consciousness being at this point synonymous. The innocence of the Garden of Eden—the womb and the "dreaming consciousness" (the phrase is Kierkegaard's) of gestation and the first month of life—is destroyed forever.

The function of psychoanalysis is to increase this consciousness, indeed to *help* people eat of the tree of the knowledge of good and evil. It should not surprise us if this experience is as terrifying for many people as it was for Oedipus. Any theory of "resistance" that omits the terror of human consciousness is incomplete and probably wrong.

In place of innocent bliss, the infant now experiences anxiety and guilt feelings. Also, part of the child's legacy is the sense of individual responsibility, and, most important of all, developing only later, the capacity to love. The "shadow" side of this process is the emergence of repressions and, concomitantly, neurosis. A fateful event indeed! If you call this the "fall of man," you should join Hegel and other penetrating analysts of history who have proclaimed that it was a "fall upward"; for without this experience there would be neither creativity nor consciousness as we know them.

But, again, *Yahweh was angry*. Adam and Eve were driven out of the garden by an angel with a flaming sword. The troublesome paradox confronts us in that both the Greek and the Judeo-Christian myths present creativity and consciousness as being born in rebellion against an omnipotent force. Are we to conclude that these chief gods, Zeus and Yahweh, did not wish humankind to have moral consciousness and the arts of civilization? It is a mystery indeed.

The most obvious explanation is that the creative artist and poet and saint must fight the *actual* (as contrasted to the ideal) gods of our society—the god of conformism as well as the gods of apathy, material success, and exploitative power. These are the "idols" of our society that are worshiped by multitudes of people. But this point does not go deeply enough to give us an answer to the riddle.

In my search for some illumination, I went back again to the myths to read them more carefully. I discovered that at the end of the myth of Prometheus there is the curious addendum: Prometheus could be freed from his chains and his torture only when an immortal would renounce his immortality as expiation for Prometheus. This was done by Chiron (who is, incidentally, another fascinating symbol—half horse and half man, renowned for his wisdom and skill in medicine and healing, he brought up Asclepius, the god of medicine). This conclusion to the myth tells us that the riddle is connected with the problem of death.

The same with Adam and Eve. Enraged at their eating of the tree of the knowledge of good and evil, Yahweh cries out that He is afraid they will eat of the tree of eternal life and become like "one of us." So! Again the riddle has to do with the problem of death, of which eternal life is one aspect.

The battle with the gods thus hinges on our own mortality! Creativity is a yearning for immortality. We human beings know that we must die. We have, strangely enough, a word for death. We know that each of us must develop the courage to confront death. Yet we also must rebel and struggle against it. Creativity comes from this struggle—out of the rebellion the creative act is born. Creativity is not merely the innocent spontaneity of our youth and childhood; it must also be married to the passion of the adult human being, which is a passion to live beyond one's death. Michelangelo's writhing, unfinished statues of slaves, struggling in their prisons of stone, are the most fitting symbol of our human condition.

8

When I use the word *rebel* for the artist, I do not refer to revolutionary or to such things as taking over the dean's office; that is a different matter. Artists are generally soft-spoken persons who are concerned with their inner visions and images. But that is precisely what makes them feared by any coercive society. For they are the bearers of the human being's age-old capacity to be insurgent. They love to immerse themselves in chaos in order to put it into form, just as God created form out of chaos in Genesis. Forever unsatisfied with the mundane, the apathetic, the conventional, they always push on to newer worlds. Thus are they the creators of the "uncreated conscience of the race."

This requires an intensity of emotion, a heightened vitality—for is not the vital forever in opposition to death? We could call this intensity by many different names: I choose to call it rage. Stanley Kunitz, contemporary poet, states that "the poet writes his poems out of his rage." This rage is necessary to ignite the poet's passion, to call forth his abilities, to bring together in ecstasy his flamelike insights, that he may surpass himself in his poems. The rage is against injustice, of which there is certainly plenty in our society. But ultimately it is rage against the prototype of all injustice—death.

We recall the first lines of a poem by another contemporary poet, Dylan Thomas, on the death of his father:

> Do not go gentle into that good night,
> Old age should burn and rave at close of day;
> Rage, rage against the dying of the light.

And the poem ends:

> And you, my father, there on the sad height,
> Curse, bless, me now with your fierce tears, I pray.
> Do not go gentle into that good night.
> Rage, rage against the dying of the light.

Note that he does not ask merely to be blessed. "Curse . . . me . . . with your *fierce* tears." Note also that it is Dylan Thomas, and not his father, who writes the poem. The father had to confront death and in some way accept it. But the son expresses the eternally insurgent spirit—and as a result we have the piercing elegance of this poem.

This rage has nothing at all to do with rational concepts of death, in which we stand outside the experience of death and make objective, statistical comments about it. That always has to do with someone else's death, not our own. We all know that each generation, whether of leaves or grass or human beings or any living things, must die in order for a new generation be born. I am speaking of death in a different sense. A child has a dog, and the dog dies. The child's grief is mixed with deep anger. If someone tries to explain death in the objective, evolutionary way to him—everything dies, and dogs die sooner that human beings —he may well strike out against the explainer. The child probably knows all that anyway. His real sense of loss and betrayal comes from the fact that his love for his dog and the dog's devotion to him are now gone. It is the personal, subjective experience of death of which I am speaking.

As we grow older we learn how to understand each other better. Hopefully, we learn also to love more authentically. Understanding and love require a wisdom that comes only with age. But at the highest point in the development of that wisdom, we will be blotted out. No longer will we see the trees turning scarlet in the autumn. No longer will we see the grass pushing up so tenderly in the spring. Each of us will become only a memory that will grow fainter every year.

This most difficult of truths is put by another modern poet, Marianne Moore, into these words:

> What is our innocence,
> what is our guilt? All are
> naked, none is safe. And whence
> is courage . . .

And then, after considering death and how we can confront it, she ends her poem:

> So he who strongly feels,
> behaves. The very bird,
>   grown taller as he sings, steels
> his form straight up. Though he is captive,
> his mighty singing
> says, satisfaction is a lowly
> thing, how pure a thing is joy.
>   This is mortality,
>   this is eternity.

Thus mortality is at last brought into antiphony with its opposite, eternity.

9

For many people the relating of rebellion to religion will be a hard truth. It brings with it the final paradox. In religion, it is not the sycophants or those who cling most faithfully to the status quo who are ultimately praised. It is the insurgents. Recall how often in human history the saint and the rebel have been the same person. Socrates was a rebel, and he was sentenced to drink hemlock. Jesus was a rebel, and he was crucified for it. Joan of Arc was a rebel, and she was burned at the stake.

Yet each of these figures and hundreds like them, though ostricized by their contemporaries, were recognized and worshiped by the following ages as having made the most significant creative contributions in ethics and religion to civilization.

Those we call saints rebelled against an outmoded and inadequate form of God on the basis of their new insights into divinity. The teachings that led to their deaths raised the ethical and spiritual levels of their societies. They were aware that Zeus, the jealous god of Mount Olympus, would no longer do. Hence Prometheus stands for a religion of compassion. They rebelled against Yahweh, the primitive tribal god of the Hebrews who gloried in the deaths of thousands of Philistines. In place of him came the new visions of Amos and Isaiah and Jeremiah of the god of love and justice. Their rebellion was motivated by new insights into the meaning of godliness. They rebelled, as Paul Tillich has so beautifully stated, against God in the name of the God beyond God. The continuous emergence of the God beyond God is the mark of creative courage in the religious sphere.

Whatever sphere we may be in, there is a profound joy in the realization that we are helping to form the structure of the new world. This is creative courage, however minor or fortuitous our creations may be. We can then say, with Joyce, Welcome, O life! We go for the millionth time to forge in the smithy of our souls the uncreated conscience of the race.

TWO

◻

THE NATURE OF
CREATIVITY

WHEN WE examine the psychological studies
and writings on creativity over the past fifty
years, the first thing that strikes us is the general
paucity of material and the inadequacy of the
work. In academic psychology after the time of
William James and during the first half of this
century, the subject was generally avoided as unscientific, mysterious, disturbing, and too corrup-
tive of the scientific training of graduate students.
And when some studies of creativity actually were
made, they dealt with areas so peripheral that
creative people themselves felt they had next to

nothing to do with real creativity. Essentially we have come up with truisms or irrelevancies at which the artists and poets smile and about which they say, "Interesting, yes. But that's not what goes on within me in the creative act." Fortunately during the last twenty years a change has been occurring, but it is still true that creativity is a stepchild of psychology.

And in psychoanalysis and depth psychology the situation has been little better. I well recall an incident of some twenty years ago that brought vividly home to me the oversimplification and inadequacy of the depth-psychology theories of creativity. One summer I was traveling with a group of seventeen artists through central Europe, studying and painting peasant art. While we were in Vienna, Alfred Adler, whom I had known and whose summer school I had attended, invited us all to his home for a private lecture. In the course of his lecture, in his parlor, Adler touched upon his *compensatory theory of creativity*—that human beings produce art, science, and other aspects of culture to compensate for their own inadequacies. The oyster producing the pearl to cover up the grain of sand intruding into its shell is often cited as a simple illustration. Beethoven's deafness was one of the many famous examples Adler cited, showing how highly creative individuals compensate for some defect or organ inferiority by their creative acts. Adler also believed that civilization was created by human beings to compensate for their relatively weak position on this unfriendly crust of earth as well as for their inadequacy of tooth and claw in the animal world. Then Adler, having entirely forgotten he was addressing a group of artists, looked around the room and remarked, "Since I see that very few of you are wearing glasses, I assume that you are not interested in art." The oversimplification this theory of compensation is subject to was thus dramatically exposed.

The theory does have some merit and is one of the important hypotheses that must be considered by students in the field. But its error is that it does not deal with *the creative process as such*. Compensatory trends in an individual will influence the forms his or her creating will take, but they do not explain the process of creativity itself. Compensatory needs influence the particular *bent* or direction in culture or science, but they do not explain the *creation* of the culture or science.

Because of this I learned very early in my psychological career to regard with a good deal of skepticism current theories explaining creativity. And I learned always to ask the question: Does the theory deal with creativity itself, or does it deal only with some artifact, some partial, peripheral aspect, of the creative act?

The other widely current psychoanalytic theories about creativity have two characteristics. First, they are *reductive*—that is, they reduce creativity to some other process. Second, they generally make it specifically an expression of *neurotic* patterns. The usual definition of creativity in psychoanalytic circles is "regression in the service of the ego." Immediately the term *regression* indicates the reductive approach. I emphatically disagree with the implication that creativity is to be understood by reducing it to some other process, or that it is essentially an expression of neurosis.

Creativity is certainly associated with serious psychological problems in our particular culture —Van Gogh went psychotic, Gauguin seems to have been schizoid, Poe was alcoholic, and Virginia Woolf was seriously depressed. Obviously creativity and originality are associated with persons who do not fit into their culture. But this does not necessarily mean that the creativity is the *product* of the neurosis.

The association of creativity with neurosis presents us with a dilemma—namely, if by psychoanalysis we cured the artists of their neuroses would they no longer create? This dichotomy, as well as many others, arises from the reductive theories. Furthermore, if we create out of some *transfer* of affect or drive, as implied in sublimation, or if our creativity is merely the by-product of an endeavor to accomplish something else, as in compensation, does not our very creative act then have only a pseudo value? We must indeed take a strong stand against the implications, however they may creep in, that talent is a disease and creativity is a neurosis.

1. WHAT IS CREATIVITY?

When we define creativity, we must make the distinction between its pseudo forms, on the one hand—that is, creativity as a superficial aestheticism. And, on the other, its authentic form—that is, the process of *bringing something new into being*. The crucial distinction is between art as artificiality (as in "artifice" or "artful") and genuine art.

This is a distinction that artists and philosophers have struggled all through the centuries to make clear. Plato, for example, demoted his poets and his artists down to the sixth circle of reality because, he said, they deal only with appearances and not with reality itself. He was referring to art as decoration, a way of making life prettier, a dealing with semblances. But in his later, beautiful dialogue, the *Symposium*, he described what he called the *true artists*—namely, those who give birth to some new reality. These poets and other creative persons are the ones who express being itself, he held. As I would put it, these are the ones who enlarge human consciousness. Their creativity is the most basic manifestation of a man or woman fulfilling his or her own being in the world.

Now we must make the above distinction clear if our inquiries into creativity are to get below the surface. We are thus not dealing with hobbies, do-it-yourself movements, Sunday painting, or other forms of filling up leisure time. Nowhere has the meaning of creativity been more disastrously lost than in the idea that it is something you do only on week ends!

The creative process must be explored not as the product of sickness, but as representing the highest degree of emotional health, as the expression of the normal people in the act of actualizing themselves. Creativity must be seen in the work of the scientist as well as in that of the artist, in the thinker as well as in the aesthetician; and one must not rule out the extent to which it is present in captains of modern technology as well as in a mother's normal relationship with her child. Creativity, as *Webster's* rightly indicates, is basically the process of *making*, of *bringing into being*.

2. THE CREATIVE PROCESS

Let us now inquire into the nature of the creative process, and seek our answers by trying to describe as accurately as possible what actually happens in individuals at the moment of the creative act. I shall speak mostly about artists because I know them, have worked with them, and, to some extent, am one myself. This does not mean that I underestimate creativity in other activities. I assume that the following analysis of the nature of creativity will apply to all men and women during their creative moments.

The first thing we notice in a creative act is that it is an *encounter*. Artists encounter the landscape they propose to paint—they look at it, observe it from this angle and that. They are, as we say, absorbed in it. Or, in the case of abstract painters, the encounter may be with an idea, an inner vision, that in turn may be led off by the brilliant colors on the palette or the inviting rough whiteness of the canvas. The paint, the canvas, and the other materials then become a secondary part of this encounter; they are the language of it, the *media*, as we rightly put it. Or scientists confront their experiment, their laboratory task, in a similar situation or encounter.

The encounter may or may not involve voluntary effort—that is, "will power." A healthy child's play, for example, also has the essential features of encounter, and we know it is one of the important prototypes of adult creativity. The essential point is not the presence or absence of voluntary effort, but the degree of absorption, the degree of intensity (which we shall deal with in detail later); there must be a specific quality of *engagement*.

Now we come upon one important distinction between pseudo, escapist creativity on the one hand and that which is genuine on the other. *Escapist creativity is that which lacks encounter.* This was illustrated vividly to me when I worked with a young man in psychoanalysis. A talented professional, this man had rich and varied creative potentialities, but he always stopped just short of actualizing them. He would suddenly get the idea for an excellent story, would work it out in his mind to a full outline which could have then been written up without much further ado, and would relish and enjoy the ecstasy of the experience. Then he would stop there, writing down nothing at all. It was as though the experience of *seeing himself as one who was able to write, as being just about to write*, had within it what he was really seeking and brought its own reward. Hence he never actually created.

This was a fairly baffling problem to him and

to me. We had analyzed many aspects of it: his father had been a somewhat gifted writer but a failure; his mother had made much of his father's writings, but had shown only contempt for him in other realms. The young man, an only child, had been pampered and overprotected by his mother and often had been shown preference over his father—for instance, by being served special food at meals. The patient was clearly competing with his father, and faced a dire threat if he should succeed. All this and more we had analyzed in some detail. A vital link of experience, however, was missing.

One day the patient came in to announce that he had made an exciting discovery. The evening before, while reading, he had gotten his customary sudden creative flow of ideas for a story and had taken his usual pleasure in the fact. At the same time he had had a peculiar sexual feeling. He had then recalled for the first time that he had always had this sexual feeling at precisely such an abortively creative moment.

I shall not go into the complex analysis of the associations, which demonstrated that this sexual feeling was both a desire for comfort and sensual gratification of a passive sort and a desire for the unconditional admiration of any woman. I only wish to indicate that the upshot was clearly that his creative "bursts" of ideas were ways of getting admiration, gratification from his mother; that he needed to show mother and other women what a fine, gifted person he was. And once he had done that by getting the beautiful, lofty visions, he had achieved what he wanted. He was not really interested in this context in creating, but in being about to create; creativity was in the service of something quite else.

Now no matter how you may interpret the causes of this pattern, one central feature is clear —*the encounter was lacking*. Is not this the essence of escapist art? Everything is there but the encounter. And is not this the central feature of many kinds of artistic exhibitionism—what Rank calls the *artiste manqué?* We cannot make a valid distinction by saying one kind of art is neurotic and the other healthy. Who is to judge that? We can only say that in exhibitionistic, escapist forms of creativity there is no real encounter, no engagement with reality. That isn't what the young man is after; he wants to be passively accepted and admired by mother. In cases of this kind it is accurate to speak of *regression* in the negative sense. But the crucial point is that we are dealing with something quite different from creativity.

The concept of encounter also enables us to make clearer the important distinction between *talent* and *creativity*. Talent may well have its neurological correlates and can be studied as "given" to a person. A man or woman may have talent whether he or she uses it or not; talent can probably be measured in the person as such. But creativity can be seen only in the act. If we were purists, we would not speak of a "creative person," but only of *a creative act.* Sometimes, as in the case of Picasso, we have great talent and at the same time great encounter and, as a result, great creativity. Sometimes we have great talent and truncated creativity, as many people felt in the case of Scott Fitzgerald. Sometimes we have a highly creative person who seems not to have much talent. It was said of the novelist Thomas Wolfe, who was one of the highly creative figures of the American scene, that he was a "genius without talent." But he was so creative because he threw himself so completely into his material and the challenge of saying it—he was great because of the intensity of his encounter.

3. INTENSITY OF THE ENCOUNTER

This leads us to the second element in the creative act—namely, the *intensity* of the encounter. *Absorption, being caught up in, wholly involved,* and so on, are used commonly to describe the state of the artist or scientist when creating or even the child at play. By whatever name one calls it, genuine creativity is characterized by an intensity of awareness, a heightened consciousness.

Artists, as well as you and I in moments of intensive encounter, experience quite clear neurological changes. These include quickened heart beat; higher blood pressure; increased intensity and constriction of vision, with eyelids narrowed so that we can see more vividly the scene we are painting; we become oblivious to things around us (as well as to the passage of time). We experience a lessening of appetite—persons engaged in a creative act lose interest in eating at the moment, and may work right through mealtime without noticing it. Now all of these correspond to an inhibiting of the functioning of the parasympathetic division of the autonomic nervous system (which has to do with ease, comfort, nourishment) and an activation of the sympathetic nervous division. And, lo and behold, we have the same picture that Walter B. Cannon described as the "flight-fight" mechanism, the energizing of the organism for fighting or fleeing. This is the neurological correlate of what we find, in broad terms, in anxiety and fear.

But what the artist or creative scientist feels is *not* anxiety or fear; it is *joy*. I use the word in contrast to happiness or pleasure. The artist, at the moment of creating, does not experience gratification or satisfaction (though this may be the case later, after he or she has a highball or a pipe in the evening. Rather, it is *joy*, joy defined as the emotion that goes with heightened consciousness, the mood that accompanies the experience of actualizing one's own potentialities.

Now this intensity of awareness is not necessarily connected with conscious purpose or willing. It may occur in reverie or in dreams, or from so-called unconscious levels. An eminent New York professor related an illustrative story. He had been searching for a particular chemical formula for some time, but without success. One night, while he was sleeping, he had a dream in which the formula was worked out and displayed before him. He woke up, and in the darkness he excitedly wrote it down on a piece of tissue, the only thing he could find. But the next morning he could not read his own scribbling. Every night thereafter, upon going to bed, he would concentrate his hopes on dreaming the dream again. Fortunately, after some nights he did, and he then wrote the formula down for good. It was the formula he had sought and for which he received the Nobel prize.

Though not rewarded so dramatically, we have all had similar experiences. Processes of forming, making, building go on even if we are not consciously aware of them at the time. William James once said that we learn to swim in the winter and to skate in the summer. Whether you wish to interpret these phenomena in terms of some formulation of the unconscious, or prefer to follow William James in connecting them with some neurological processes that continue even when we are not working on them, or prefer some other approach, as I do, it is still clear that creativity goes on in varying degrees of intensity on levels not directly under the control of conscious willing. Hence the heightened awareness we are speaking of does not at all mean increased self-consciousness. It is rather correlated with abandon and absorption, and it involves a heightening of awareness in the whole personality.

But let it be said immediately that unconscious insights or answers to problems that come in reverie do not come hit or miss. They may indeed occur at times of relaxation, or in fantasy, or at other times when we alternate play with work. But what is entirely clear is that they pertain to those areas in which the person consciously has worked laboriously and with dedication. *Purpose* in the human being is a much more complex phenomenon that what used to be called will power. Purpose involves all levels of experience. We cannot *will* to have insights. We cannot *will* creativity. But we can *will* to give ourselves to the encounter with intensity of dedication and commitment. The deeper aspects of awareness are activated to the extent that the person is committed to the encounter.

We must also point out that this "intensity of encounter" is not to be identified with what is called the *Dionysian* aspect of creativity. You will find this word *Dionysian* used often in books on creative works. Taken from the name of the Greek god of intoxication and other forms of ecstasy, the term refers to the upsurge of vitality, the abandon, which characterized the ancient orgiastic revels of Dionysus. Nietzsche, in his important book *The Birth of Tragedy*, cites the Dionysian principle of surging vitality and the Apollonian principle of form and rational order as the two dialectical principles that operate in creativity. This dichotomy is assumed by many students and writers.

The Dionysian aspect of intensity can be studied psychoanalytically easily enough. Probably almost every artist has tried at some time or other to paint while under the influence of alcohol. What happens generally is what one would expect, and it happens in proportion to how much alcohol is consumed—namely, that the artist *thinks* he or she is doing wonderful stuff, indeed much better than usual, but in actual fact, as is noted the next morning while looking at the picture, has really performed less well than usual. Certainly Dionysian periods of abandon are valuable, particularly in our mechanized civilization where creativity and the arts are all but starved to death by the routine of punching clocks and attending endless committee meetings, and by the pressures to produce ever greater quantities of papers and books, pressures that have infested the academic world more lethally than the industrial world. I long for the health-giving effects of the periods of "carnival," such as they still have in the Mediterranean countries.

But the intensity of the creative act should be *related to the encounter objectively*, and not released merely by something the artist "takes." Alcohol is a depressant, and possibly necessary in an industrial civilization; but when one needs it regularly to feel free of inhibitions, he or she is misnaming the problem. The issue really is why the inhibitions are there in the first place. The psychological studies of the upsurge of vitality and other effects that occur when such drugs are taken are exceedingly interesting; but one must sharply distinguish this from the intensity that accompanies the encounter itself. The encounter is not something that occurs merely because we ourselves have subjectively changed; it represents, rather, a real relationship with the objective world.

The important and profound aspect of the Dionysian principle is that of *ecstasy*. It was in connection with Dionysian revels that Greek drama was developed, a magnificent summit of creativity which achieved a union of *form and passion* with *order and vitality. Ecstasy* is the technical term for the process in which this union occurs.

The topic of ecstasy is one to which we should give more active attention in psychology. I use the word, of course, not in its popular and cheapened sense of "hysteria," but in its historical, etymological sense of "ex-stasis"—that is, literally to "stand out from," to be freed from the usual split between subject and object which is a perpetual dichotomy in most human activity. *Ecstasy* is the accurate term for the intensity of consciousness that occurs in the creative act. But it is not to be thought of merely as a Bacchic "letting go"; it involves the total person, with the subconscious and unconscious acting in unity with the conscious. It is not, thus, *irrational*; it is, rather, suprarational. It brings intellectual, volitional, and emotional functions into play all together.

What I am saying may sound strange in the light of our traditional academic psychology. It *should* sound strange. Our traditional psychology has been founded on the dichotomy between subject and object which has been the central characteristic of Western thought for the past four centuries. Ludwig Binswanger calls this dichotomy "the cancer of all psychology and psychiatry up to now."[1] It is not avoided by behaviorism or operationalism, which would define experience only in objective terms. Nor is it avoided by isolating the creative experience as a purely subjective phenomenon.

Most psychological and other modern schools of thought still assume this split without being aware of it. We have tended to set reason over against emotions, and have assumed, as an outgrowth of this dichotomy, that we could observe something most accurately if our emotions were not involved—that is to say, we would be least biased if we had no emotional stake at all in the matter at hand. I think this is an egregious error. There are now data in Rorschach responses, for example, that indicate that people can more accurately observe precisely when they are emotionally involved—that is, reason works better when emotions are present; the person sees sharper and more accurately when his emotions are engaged. Indeed, we cannot really see an object unless we have some emotional involvement with it. It may well be that reason works best in the state of ecstasy.

The Dionysian and the Apollonian must be related to each other. Dionysian vitality rests on this question: What manner of encounter releases the vitality? What particular relation to landscape or inner vision or idea heightens the consciousness, brings forth the intensity?

4. ENCOUNTER AS INTERRELATING
WITH THE WORLD

We arrive finally in analyzing the creative act in terms of the question What is this intense encounter *with?* An encounter is always a meeting between two poles. The subjective pole is the conscious person in the creative act itself. But what is the objective pole of this dialectical relationship? I shall use a term that will sound too simple: it is the artist's or scientist's encounter with his *world.* I do not mean world as environment or as the "sum total" of things; nor do I refer at all to objects about a subject.

World is the pattern of meaningful relations in which a person exists and in the design of which he or she participates. It has objective reality, to be sure, but it is not simply that. World is interrelated with the person at every moment. A continual dialectical process goes on between world and self and self and world; one implies the other, and neither can be understood if we omit the other. This is why one can never localize creativity as a *subjective* phenomenon; one can never study it simply in terms of what goes on within the person. The pole of world is an inseparable part of the creativity of an individual. What occurs is always a *process,* a *doing*—specifically a process interrelating the person and his or her world.

How artists encounter their world is illustrated in the work of every genuinely creative painter. Out of the many possible examples of this, I shall choose the superb exhibition of the paintings of Mondrian shown at the Guggenheim Museum in New York in 1957–58. From his first realistic works in 1904 and 1905, all the way to his later geometrical rectangles and squares in the 1930s, one can see him struggling to find the underlying forms of the objects, particularly trees, that he was painting. He seems to have loved trees. The paintings around 1910, beginning somewhat like Cézanne, move further and further into the underlying meaning of tree—the trunk rises organically from the ground into which the roots have penetrated; the branches curve and bend into the trees and hills of the background in cubistic form, beautifully illustrative of what the underlying essence of tree is to most of us. Then we see Mondrian struggling more and more deeply to find the "ground forms" of nature, now it is less tree and more the eternal geometric forms underlying all reality. Finally we see him pushing inexorably toward the squares and rectangles that are the ultimate form of purely abstract art. Impersonal? To be sure. The individual self is lost. But is this not precisely a reflection of Mondrian's world—the world of the decades of the twenties and thirties, the world in the period of emerging fascism, communism, conformism, military power, in which the individual not only feels lost, but *is* lost, alienated from nature and others as well as himself? Mondrian's paintings express creative strength *in* such a world, an affirmation in spite of the "lostness" of the individual. In this sense his work is a search for the foundation of individuality that can withstand these antihuman political developments.

It is absurd to think of artists simply as "painting nature," as though they were only anachronistic photographers of trees and lakes and mountains. For them, nature is a medium, a language by which they reveal their world. What genuine painters do is to reveal the underlying psychological and spiritual conditions of their relationship to their world; thus in the works of a great painter we have a reflection of the emotional and spiritual condition of human beings in that period of history. If you wish to understand the psychological and spiritual temper of any historical period, you can do no better than to look long and searchingly at its art. For in the art the underlying spiritual meaning of the period is expressed directly in symbols. This is not because artists are didactic or set out to teach or to make propaganda; to the extent that they do, their power of expression is broken; their direct relation to the inarticulate, or, if you will, "unconscious" levels of the culture is destroyed. They have the power to reveal the underlying meaning of any period precisely because the essence of art is the powerful and alive encounter between the artist and his or her world.

Nowhere was this encounter demonstrated more vividly than in the famous seventy-fifth anniversary exhibit of Picasso's works, presented in New York in 1957. Broader in temperament than Mondrian, Picasso is a spokesman for his time *par excellence*. Even in his early works around 1900, his vast talent was already visible. And in the stark, realistic paintings of peasants and poor people in the first decade of this century, his passionate relationship to human suffering was shown. You can then see the spiritual temper of each succeeding decade in his work.

In the early 1920s, for example, we find Picasso painting classical Greek figures, particularly bathers by the sea. An aura of escapism hovers about these pictures in the exhibit. Was not the 1920s, the decade after the first World War, in reality a period of escapism in the Western world? Toward the end of the twenties and in the early thirties, these bathers by the sea become pieces of metal, mechanical, gray-blue curving steel. Beautiful indeed, but impersonal, unhuman. And here one was gripped in the exhibit with an ominous foreboding—the prediction of the beginning of the time when people were to become impersonal, objectivized, numbers. It was the ominous prediction of the beginnings of "man, the robot."

Then in 1937 comes the great painting *Guernica,* with figures torn apart, split from each other, all in stark white, gray, and black. It was Picasso's pained outrage against the inhumanity of the bombing of the helpless Spanish town of Guernica by fascist planes in the Spanish revolution; but it is much more than that. It is the most vivid portrayal imaginable of the atomistic, split-up, fragmentized state of contemporary human beings, and implies the conformism, emptiness, and despair that were to go along with this. Then in the late thirties and forties, Picasso's portraits become more and more machinelike— people turned literally into metal. Faces become distorted. It is as though persons, individuals, do not exist any more; their places are taken by hideous witches. Pictures now are not *named,* but *numbered.* The bright colors the artist used in his earlier periods and which were so delightful are now largely gone. In these rooms at the exhibit one feels as though darkness has settled upon the earth at noon. As in the novels of Kafka, one gets a stark and gripping feeling of the modern individual's loss of humanity. The first time I saw this exhibit, I was so overcome with the foreboding picture of human beings losing their faces, their individuality, their humanity, and the prediction of the robot to come, that I could look no longer and had to hurry out of the room and onto the street again.

To be sure, all the way through Picasso preserves his own sanity by "playing" with paintings and sculptures of animals and his own children. But it is clear that the main stream is a portrayal of our modern condition, which has been psychologically portrayed by Riesman, Mumford, Tillich, and others. The whole is an unforgettable portrait of modern man and woman in the process of losing their person and their humanity.

In this sense genuine artists are so bound up with their age that they cannot communicate separated from it. In this sense, too, the historical situation conditions the creativity. For the consciousness which obtains in creativity is not the superficial level of objectified intellectualization, but is an encounter with the world on a level that undercuts the subject-object split. "Creativity," to rephrase our definition, "is the encounter of the intensively conscious human being with his or her world."

THREE

□

CREATIVITY AND
THE UNCONSCIOUS

EVERYONE uses from time to time such expressions as, "a thought pops up," an idea comes "from the blue" or "dawns" or "comes as though out of a dream," or "it suddenly hit me." These are various ways of describing a common experience: the breakthrough of ideas from some depth below the level of awareness. I shall call this realm "the unconscious" as a catchall for the subconscious, preconscious, and other dimensions below awareness.

When I use the phrase "the unconscious," I, of course, mean it as a shorthand. There is no such thing as *"the* unconscious"; it is, rather, unconscious dimensions (or aspects or sources) of experience. I define this unconscious as *the potentialities for awareness or action which the individual cannot or will not actualize.* These potentialities are the source of what can be called "free creativity." The exploration of unconscious phenomena has a fascinating relationship to creativity. What are the nature and characteristics of the creativity that has its source in these unconscious depths of personality?

1

I wish to begin our exploration of this topic by relating an incident from my own experience. When I was a graduate student doing research on *The Meaning of Anxiety,* I studied anxiety in a group of unmarried mothers—i.e., pregnant young women in their late teens and early twenties in a shelter home in New York City.[1] I had a good, sound hypothesis on anxiety, approved by my professors and approved by me—that the predisposition toward anxiety in individuals would be proportionate to the degree to which they had been rejected by their mothers. In psychoanalysis and psychology this had been a generally accepted hypothesis. I assumed the anxiety of people like these young women would be cued off by the anxiety-creating situation of being unwed and pregnant, and I could then study more openly the original source of their anxiety—namely the maternal rejection.

Now I discovered that half the young women fitted my hypothesis beautifully. But the other half did not fit it at all. This latter group included young women from Harlem and the Lower East Side who had been radically rejected by their mothers. One of them, whom I shall call Helen, was from a family of twelve children whose mother drove them out of the house on the first day of summer to stay with their father, the care-taker of a barge that went up and down the Hudson River. Helen was pregnant by her father. At the time she was in the shelter, he was in Sing Sing on a charge of rape by Helen's older sister. Like the other young women of this group, Helen would say to me, "We have troubles, but we don't worry."

This was a very curious thing to me and I had a hard time believing the data. But the facts seemed clear. As far as I could tell by the Ror-schach, TAT, and other tests I used, these radically rejected young women did not carry any unusual degree of anxiety. Forced out of the house by their mothers, they simply made their friends among other youngsters on the street.

Hence, there was not the predisposition to anxiety we would have expected according to what we know in psychology.

How could this be? Had the rejected young women who had not experienced anxiety become hardened, apathetic, so that they did not feel the rejection? The answer to that seemed clearly no. Were they psychopathic or sociopathic types, who also don't experience anxiety? Again, no. I felt myself caught by an insoluble problem.

Late one day, putting aside my books and papers in the little office I used in that shelter house, I walked down the street toward the subway. I was tired. I tried to put the whole troublesome business out of my mind. About fifty feet away from the entrance to the Eighth Street station, it suddenly struck me "out of the blue," as the not-unfitting expression goes, that those young women who didn't fit my hypothesis *were all from the proletarian class*. And as quickly as that idea struck me, other ideas poured out. I think I had not taken another step on the sidewalk when a whole new hypothesis broke loose in my mind. I realized my entire theory would have to be changed. I saw at that instant that it is not rejection by the mother that is the original trauma which is the source of anxiety; it is rather *rejection that is lied about.*

The proletarian mothers rejected their children,

but they never made any bones about it. The children knew they were rejected; they went out on the streets and found other companions. There was never any subterfuge about their situation. They knew their world—bad or good—and they could orient themselves to it. But the middle-class young women were always lied to in their families. They were rejected by mothers who pretended they loved them. This was really the source of their anxiety, not the sheer rejection. I saw, in that instantaneous way that characterizes insights from these deeper sources, that anxiety comes from *not being able to know the world you're in, not being able to orient yourself in your own existence.* I was convinced there, on the street—and later thought and experience only convinced me the more—that this is a better, more accurate, and more elegant theory, than my first.

2

What was going on at the moment when this breakthrough occurred? Taking this experience of mine as a start, we notice, first of all, that the insight broke into my conscious mind *against* what I had been trying to think rationally. I had a good, sound thesis and I had been working very hard trying to prove it. The unconscious, so to speak, *broke through in opposition to the conscious belief to which I was clinging.*

Carl Jung often made the point that there is a polarity, a kind of opposition, between unconscious experience and consciousness. He believed the relationship was compensatory: consciousness controls the wild, illogical vagaries of the unconscious, while the unconscious keeps consciousness from drying up in banal, empty, arid rationality. The compensation also works on specific problems: if I consciously bend too far one way on some issue, my unconscious will lean the other way. This is, of course, the reason why the more we are unconsciously smitten with doubts about an idea, the more dogmatically we fight for it in our conscious arguments. This is also why persons as different as Saint Paul on the Damascus road and the alcoholic in the Bowery go through such radical conversions—the repressed unconscious side of the dialectic erupts and takes over the personality. The unconscious seems to take delight (if I may so express it) in breaking through—and breaking up—exactly what we cling to most rigidly in our conscious thinking.

What occurs in this breakthrough is not simply growth; it is much more dynamic. It is not a mere expansion of awareness; it is rather a kind of battle. A dynamic struggle goes on within a person between what he or she consciously thinks on the one hand and, on the other, some insight, some perspective that is struggling to be born. The insight is then born with anxiety, guilt, and the joy and gratification that is inseparable from the actualizing of a new idea or vision.

The guilt that is present when this breakthrough occurs has its source in the fact that the insight must destroy something. My insight destroyed my other hypothesis and would destroy what a number of my professors believed, a fact that caused me some concern. Whenever there is a breakthrough of a significant idea in science or a significant new form in art, the new idea will destroy what a lot of people believe is essential to the survival of their intellectual and spiritual world. This is the source of guilt in genuine creative work. As Picasso remarked, "Every act of creation is first of all an act of destruction."

The breakthrough carries with it also an element of anxiety. For it not only broke down my previous hypothesis, it shook my self-world relationship. At such a time I find myself having to seek a new foundation, the existence of which I as yet don't know. This is the source of the anxious feeling that comes at the moment of the breakthrough; it is not possible that there be a genuinely new idea without this shake up occurring to some degree.

But beyond guilt and anxiety, as I said above,

the main feeling that comes with the break-through is one of gratification. We have seen something new. We have the joy of participating in what the physicists and other natural scientists call an experience of "elegance."

3

A second thing that occurred in the breakthrough of this insight is that *everything around me became suddenly vivid.* I can remember that on the particular street down which I walked the houses were painted an ugly shade of green that I normally would prefer to forget immediately. But by virtue of the vividness of this experience, the colors all around were sharpened and were imbedded in my experience, and that ugly green still exists in my memory. The moment the insight broke through, there was a special translucence that enveloped the world, and my vision was given a special clarity. I am convinced that this is the usual accompaniment of the breakthrough of unconscious experience into consciousness. Here is again part of the reason the experience scares us so much: the world, both inwardly and outwardly, takes on an intensity that may be momentarily overwhelming. This is one aspect of what is called ecstasy—the uniting of unconscious experience with consciousness, a union that is not *in abstracto,* but a dynamic, immediate fusion.

I want to emphasize that I did not get my insight as though I were dreaming, with the world and myself opaque and cloudy. It is a popular misconception that perception is dull when one is experiencing this state of insight. I believe that perception is actually sharper. True, one aspect of it resembles a dream in that self and world may become kaleidoscopic; but another aspect of the experience is a sharpened perception, a vividness, a translucence of relationship to the things around us. The world becomes vivid and unforgettable. Thus the breakthrough of material from unconscious dimensions involves a heightening of sensory experience.

We could, indeed, define the whole experience that we are talking about as *a state of heightened consciousness.* Unconsciousness is the depth dimension of consciousness, and when it surges up into consciousness in this kind of polar struggle the result is an intensification of consciousness. It heightens not only the capacity to think, but also the sensory processes; and it certainly intensifies memory.

There is a third thing we observe when such insights occur—that is, *the insight never comes hit or miss, but in accordance with a pattern of which one essential element is our own commitment.* The breakthrough does not come by just "taking it easy," by "letting the unconscious do it." The insight, rather, is born from unconscious levels exactly in the areas in which we are most intensively consciously committed. The insight came to me on that problem to which, up till the moment I put my books and papers away in the little office that I occupied, I had devoted my best and most energetic conscious thought. The idea, the new form which suddenly becomes present, *came in order to complete an incomplete Gestalt with which I was struggling in conscious awareness*. One can quite accurately speak of this incomplete Gestalt, this unfinished pattern, this unformed form, as constituting the "call" that was answered by the unconscious.

The fourth characteristic of this experience is that *the insight comes at a moment of transition between work and relaxation*. It comes at a break in periods of voluntary effort. My breakthrough came when I had put away my books and was walking toward the subway, my mind far away from that problem. It is as though intense application to the problem—thinking about it, struggling with it—starts and keeps the work process going; but some part of the pattern that is different from what I am trying to work out is struggling to be born. Hence the tension that is involved in creative activity. If we are too rigid, dogmatic, or bound to previous conclusions, we will, of course, never let this new element come into our consciousness; we will never let ourselves be aware of the knowledge that exists on another level within us. But the insight often cannot be born until the conscious tension, the conscious application, is relaxed. Hence the well-known phenomenon that the unconscious breakthrough requires the alternation of intense, conscious work and relaxation, with the unconscious insight often occurring, as in my case, at the moment of the shift.

Albert Einstein once asked a friend of mine in Princeton, "Why is it I get my best ideas in the morning while I'm shaving?" My friend answered, as I have been trying to say here, that often the mind needs the relaxation of inner controls— needs to be freed in reverie or day dreaming— for the unaccustomed ideas to emerge.

4

Let us now consider the experience, more complex and richer than mine, of one of the great mathematicians of the late nineteenth and early twentieth centuries, Jules Henri Poincaré. In his autobiography, Poincaré tells us with admirable clarity how his new insights and new theories came to him, and he describes vividly the circumstances surrounding the occurrence of one "breakthrough."

For fifteen days I strove to prove that there could not be any functions like those I have since called Fuchsian functions. I was then very ignorant; every day I seated myself at my work table, stayed an hour or two, tried a great number of combinations and reached no results. One evening, contrary to my custom, I drank black coffee and could not sleep. Ideas rose in crowds; I felt them collide until pairs interlocked, so to speak, making a stable combination. By the next morning I had established the existence of a class of Fuchsian functions, those which come from the hypergeometric series; I had only to write out the results, which took but a few hours.[2]

Still a young man, he was then called into the military service, and for some months nothing happened in his thinking. One day in a town in southern France he was getting on a bus and talking with another soldier. As he was about to put his foot on the step—he pinpoints the moment that exactly—there broke into his mind the answer to how these new mathematical functions that he had discovered were related to the conventional mathematics he had been working on before. When I read Poincaré's experience— which was after the above incident in my own life—I was struck by how similar it was in this special precision and vividness. He got up on the step, entered the bus, continued without pause his conversation with his friend, but was completely and instantaneously convinced of the way these functions were related to general mathematics.

To continue with a later portion of his autobiography, when he returned from army service:

Then I turned my attention to the study of some arithmetical questions apparently without much success and without a suspicion of any connection with my preceding researches. Disgusted with my failure, I went to spend a few days at the seaside, and thought of something else. One morning, walking on the bluff, the idea came to me, with just the same characteristics of brevity, suddenness and immediate certainty, that the arithmetic transformations of indeterminate ternary quadratic forms were identical with those of non-Euclidean geometry.[3]

Poincaré, turning psychologist for the moment, asks himself the question we posed above: What is going on in the mind that these ideas should break through at this moment? This is what he proposes in answer to his question:

Most striking at first is this appearance of sudden illumination, a manifest sign of long, unconscious prior work. The role of this unconscious work in mathematical invention appears to me incontestable, and traces of it would be found in other cases where it is less evident. Often when one works at a hard question, nothing good is accomplished at the first attack. Then one takes a rest, longer or shorter, and sits down anew to the work. During the first half-hour, as before, nothing is found, and then all of a sudden the decisive idea presents itself to the mind. It might be said that the conscious work has been more fruitful because it has been interrupted and the rest has given back to the mind its force and freshness.[4]

Is the appearance of the illumination due to the relief from fatigue—i.e., simply taking a rest? No, he answers:

It is more probable that this rest has been filled out with unconscious work and that the result of this work has afterward revealed itself to the geometer just as in the cases I have cited; only the revelation, instead of coming during a walk or a journey, has happened during a period of conscious work, but independently of this work which plays at most a role of excitant, as if it were the goad stimulating the results already reached during rest, but remaining unconscious, to assume the conscious form.[5]

He then continues with another penetrating comment on the practical aspects of the breakthrough:

There is another remark to be made about the conditions of this unconscious work: it is possible, and of a certainty it is only fruitful, if it is on the one hand preceded and on the other hand followed by a period of conscious work. These sudden inspirations (and the examples already cited sufficiently prove this) never happen except after some days of voluntary effort which has appeared absolutely fruitless and whence nothing good seems to have come, where the way taken seems totally astray. These efforts then have not been as sterile as one thinks; they have set agoing the unconscious machine and without them it would not have moved and would have produced nothing.[6]

Let us summarize some of the most significant

points so far in Poincaré's testimony. He sees the characteristics of the experience as follows: (1) the *suddenness* of the illumination; (2) that the insight may occur, and to some extent *must* occur, *against* what one has clung to consciously in one's theories; (3) the *vividness* of the incident and the whole scene that surrounds it; (4) the *brevity* and *conciseness* of the insight, along with the experience of *immediate certainty*. Continuing with the practical conditions which he cites as necessary for this experience are (5) hard work on the topic *prior to the breakthrough*; (6) a *rest*, in which the "unconscious work" has been given a chance to proceed on its own and after which the breakthrough may occur (which is a special case of the more general point); (7) the necessity of *alternating work and relaxation*, with the insight often coming at the moment of the break between the two, or at least within the break.

This last point is particularly interesting. It is probably something everyone has learned: professors will lecture with more inspiration if they occasionally alternate the classroom with the beach; authors will write better when, as Macaulay used to do, they write for two hours, then pitch quoits, and then go back to their writing. But certainly more than the mere mechanical alternation is involved.

I propose that in our day this alternation of

the market place and mountain requires the capacity for the *constructive use of solitude*. It requires that we be able to retire from a world that is "too much with us," that we be able to be quiet, that we let the solitude work for us and in us. It is a characteristic of our time that many people are afraid of solitude: to be alone is a sign one is a social failure, for no one would be alone if he or she could help it. It often occurs to me that people living in our modern, hectic civilization, amid the constant din of radio and TV, subjecting themselves to every kind of stimulation whether of the passive sort of TV or the more active sort of conversation, work, and activity, that people with such constant preoccupations find it exceedingly difficult to let insights from unconscious depths break through. Of course, when an individual is afraid of the irrational—that is, of the unconscious dimensions of experience—he tries to keep busiest, tries to keep the most "noise" going on about him. The avoidance of the anxiety of solitude by constant agitated diversion is what Kierkegaard, in a nice simile, likened to the settlers in the early days of America who used to beat on pots and pans at night to make enough din to keep the wolves away. Obviously if we are to experience insights from our unconscious, we need to be able to give ourselves to solitude.

Poincaré finally asks: What determines *why* a

given idea comes through from the unconscious? Why this particular insight and not one of a dozen others? Is it because a particular insight is the answer which is empirically most accurate? No, he answers. Is it because it is the insight which will pragmatically work best? Again, no. What Poincaré proposes as the selective factor resulting in this given insight seems to me to be in some ways the most important and gripping point in his whole analysis:

The useful combinations [that come through from the unconscious] are precisely the most beautiful, I mean those best able to charm this special sensibility that all mathematicians know, but of which the profane are so ignorant as often to be tempted to smile at it.
. . . Among the great numbers of combinations blindly formed by the subliminal self, almost all are without interest and without utility; but just for that reason they are also without effect upon the esthetic sensibility. Consciousness will never know them; only certain ones are harmonious, and, consequently, at once useful and beautiful. They will be capable of touching this special sensibility of the geometer of which I have just spoken, and which, once aroused, will call our attention to them, and thus give them occasion to become conscious.[7]

This is why the mathematicians and physicists talk about the "elegance" of a theory. The utility is subsumed as part of the character of being beautiful. The harmony of an internal form, the inner consistency of a theory, the character of beauty that touches one's sensibilities—these are significant factors determining why a given idea emerges. As a psychoanalyst, I can only add that my experience in helping people achieve insights reveals the same phenomenon—that insights emerge not chiefly because they are "rationally true" or even helpful, but because they have a certain form, the form that is beautiful because it completes an incomplete Gestalt.

When this breakthrough of a creative insight into consciousness occurs, we have the subjective conviction that the form should be this way and no other way. It is characteristic of the creative experience that it strikes us as true—with the "immediate certainty" of Poincaré. And we think, nothing else could have been true in that situation, and we wonder why we were so stupid as not to have seen it earlier. The reason, of course, is that we were not psychologically ready to see it. We could not yet *intend* the new truth or creative form in art or scientific theory. We were not yet open on the level of intentionality. But the "truth" itself is simply there. This reminds us of what the Zen Buddhists keep saying—that at these moments is reflected and revealed a reality of the universe that does not depend merely on our own subjectivity, but is as though we only had our eyes closed and suddenly we open them and there it is, as simple as can be. The new reality has a kind of immutable, eternal quality. The experience that "this is the way reality is and isn't it strange we didn't see it sooner" may have a religious quality with artists. This is why many artists feel that something holy is going on when they paint, that there is something in the act of creating which is like a religious revelation.

5

We now consider some dilemmas which arise from the relation of the unconscious to techniques and machines. No discussion of creativity and the unconscious in our society can possibly avoid these difficult and important problems.

We live in a world that has become mechanized to an amazingly high degree. Irrational unconscious phenomena are always a threat to this mechanization. Poets may be delightful creatures in the meadow or the garret, but they are menaces on the assembly line. Mechanization requires uniformity, predictability, and orderliness; and the very fact that unconscious phenomena are original and irrational is already an inevitable threat to bourgeois order and uniformity.

This is one reason people in our modern Western civilization have been afraid of unconscious and irrational experience. For the potentialities that surge up in them from deeper mental wells simply don't fit the technology which has become so essential for our world. What people today do out of fear of irrational elements in themselves as well as in other people is *to put tools and mechanics between themselves and the unconscious world.* This protects them from being grasped by the frightening and threatening aspects of irrational experience. I am saying nothing whatever, I am sure it will be understood, against technology or techniques or mechanics in themselves. What I am saying is that the danger always exists that our technology will serve as a buffer between us and nature, a block between us and the deeper dimensions of our own experience. Tools and techniques ought to be an *extension* of consciousness, but they can just as easily be a *protection* from consciousness. Then tools become defense mechanisms—specifically against the wider and more complex dimensions of consciousness that we call the unconscious. Our mechanisms and technology then make us "uncertain in the impulses of the spirit," as the physicist Heisenberg puts it.[8]

Western civilization since the Renaissance has centrally emphasized techniques and mechanics. Thus it is understandable that the creative impulses of ourselves and our forefathers, again since the Renaissance, should have been channeled into the making of technical things—

creativity directed toward the advance and application of science. Such channeling of creativity into technical pursuits is appropriate on one level but serves as a psychological defense on a deeper level. This means that technology will be clung to, believed in, and depended on far beyond its legitimate sphere, since it also serves as a defense against our fears of irrational phenomena. Thus the very success of technological creativity—and that its success is magnificent does not need to be heralded by me—is a threat to its own existence. For if we are not open to the unconscious, irrational, and transrational aspects of creativity, then our science and technology have helped to block us off from what I shall call "creativity of the spirit." By this I mean creativity that has nothing to do with technical use; I mean creativity in art, poetry, music, and other areas that exist for our delight and the deepening and enlarging of meaning in our lives rather than for making money or for increasing technical power.

To the extent that we lose this free, original creativity of the spirit as it is exemplified in poetry and music and art, we shall also lose our scientific creativity. Scientists themselves, particularly the physicists, have told us that the creativity of science is bound up with the freedom of human beings to create in the free, pure sense. In modern physics it is very clear that the discoveries that later become utilized for our technological gains are generally made in the first place because a physicist lets his imagination go and discovers something simply for the joy of discovery. But this always runs the risk of radically upsetting our previously nicely worked-out theories, as it did when Einstein introduced his theory of relativity, and Heisenberg introduced his principle of indeterminacy. My point here is more than the conventional distinction between "pure" and "applied" science. The creativity of the spirit *does* and *must* threaten the structure and presuppositions of our rational, orderly society and way of life. Unconscious, irrational urges are bound by their very nature to be a threat to our rationality, and the anxiety we experience thereupon is inescapable.

I am proposing that the creativity coming from the preconscious and unconscious is not only important for art and poetry and music; but is essential in the long run also for our science. To shrink from the anxiety this entails, and block off the threatening new insights and forms this engenders, is not only to render our society banal and progressively more empty, but also to cut off as well the headwaters in the rough and rocky mountains of the stream that later becomes the river of creativity in our science. The new physicists and mathematicians, for fairly obvious reasons, have been furthest ahead in realizing this interrelation between unconscious, irrational illumination and scientific discovery.

Let me now give an illustration of the problem we face. In the several times I have been on television, I have been struck by two different feelings. One was wonder at the fact that my words, spoken in the studio, could be delivered instantaneously into the living rooms of half a million people. The other was that whenever I got an original idea, whenever in these programs I began to struggle with some unformed, new concept, whenever I had an original thought that might cross some frontier of the discussion, at that point I was cut off. I have no resentment against emcees who do this; they know their business, and they realize that if what goes on in the program does not fit in the world of listeners all the way from Georgia to Wyoming, the viewers will get up, go to the kitchen, get a beer, come back, and switch on a Western.

When you have the potentialities for tremendous mass communication, you inevitably tend to communicate on the level of the half-million people who are listening. What you say must have some place in their world, must at least be partly known to them. Inevitably, then, originality, the breaking of frontiers, the radical newness of ideas and images are at best dubious and at worst totally unacceptable. Mass communication—wonder as it may be technologically and something to be appreciated and valued—presents us with a serious danger, the danger of conformism, due to the fact that we all view the same things at the same time in all the cities of the country. This very fact throws considerable weight on the side of regularity and uniformity and against originality and freer creativity.

6

Just as the poet is a menace to conformity, he is also a constant threat to political dictators. He is always on the verge of blowing up the assembly line of political power.

We have had powerful and poignant demonstrations of this in Soviet Russia. It appeared chiefly in the prosecution and purge of artists and writers under Stalin, who was pathologically anxious when faced with the threat that the creative unconscious posed to his political system. Indeed, some students believe that the present situation in Russia shows an ongoing struggle between rationality and what we have been calling "free creativity." George Reavey, in his introduction to the work of the Russian poet Yevgeny Yevtushenko writes:

There is something about the poet and his poetic utterance that has a terrifying effect on some Russians, and especially on the Authorities, be they Tzarist or Soviet. It is as though *poetry were an irrational force which must be bridled and subjugated and even destroyed.*[9]

Reavey cites the tragic fate that has befallen so many Russian poets, and suggests that "it is as though Russia were frightened by the expanding image of its culture and, feeling threatened by the possible loss of its own simple theoretical identity, must needs shatter anything more complex as something alien to itself." He feels that this "may be due to an inherent strain of puritanism. Or to the reaction of an archaic form of despotic paternalism." Or to the present painful effects of a too sudden transition from serfdom to industrialization. I would also raise the question as to whether there is among Russians less cultural and psychological defense against irrational elements in themselves and their society than among people of other nations. Don't Russians, in fact, live closer to irrational elements than the older European countries, and, therefore, being more threatened by untamed irrationality, have to make a greater effort to control it by regulation?

Could not the same question be fruitfully raised about the United States—that is, are not our emphasis on pragmatic rationalism, our practical controls, and our behavioristic ways of thinking defenses against the irrational elements that were present on the frontiers of our society only a hundred years ago? These irrational elements are always bursting out—often to our considerable embarrassment—in the prairie fires of revival movements of the nineteenth century, in the Ku Klux Klan, and in McCarthyism, to name mainly negative examples.

But there is a special point I'd like to make here about preoccupation in the United States with "behavior." The sciences of man in America are called *"behavioral* sciences," the American Psychological Association's national television program was called "Accent on *Behavior,"* and our chief original and only extensive contribution to psychological schools is *behaviorism,* in contrast to the many European schools—psychoanalysis, Gestalt structuralism, existential psychology, etc. Practically all of us as children have heard: "Behave yourself! Behave! Behave!" The relation between moralistic puritanism and this preoccupation with behavior is by no means entirely fictitious or accidental. Is not our emphasis on behavior a carry-over of *our* "inherent strain of puritanism," as Reavey suggests may be the case in Russia? I am, of course, entirely aware of the argument that we have to study behavior because that's the only thing that can be studied with any kind of objectivity. But this could well be—and I propose it is—a parochial prejudice raised to the level of a scientific principle. If we accept it as a presupposition, does it not lead to the greatest mistake of all, from the point of view of this chapter—namely, a denial by fiat of the significance of irrational, subjective activity by subsuming it under the guise of its external results?

In any case, Reavey states that even though Stalin is dead, the situation of the poet in Russia is still precarious because the younger poets and some of the hitherto muzzled older poets have become more determined to express their real feelings and to interpret the truth as they see it. These poets have not only been condemning the corrupt substitution of falsehood for truth in Russia, but are trying to rejuvenate the language of Russian poetry by clearing it of political clichés and "father images." During Stalinism this was condemned as "ideological co-existence" with the "bourgeois world," and the poet was cut down for anything that "seemed to endanger the closed, exclusive system of Soviet Realism." The only trouble is, any kind of "closed, exclusive system" destroys poetry as it does all art. Reavey continues:

In a speech pronounced in 1921, Alexander Blok, the great Russian poet, had argued that "tranquility and freedom" were "essential to the poet in order to set harmony free." But he went on to say, "the Soviet authorities also take away our tranquility and freedom. *Not outward but creative tranquility.* Not the childish do-as-you-will, not the freedom to play the liberal, but *the creative will*—the secret freedom. And the poet is dying, because there is no longer anything to breathe; life has lost its meaning for him."[10]

This is a powerful statement of my thesis— namely, that a *sine qua non* of creativity is the freedom of artists to give all the elements within themselves free play in order to open up the possibility of what Blok excellently calls "the creative will."[11] The negative part of Blok's statement is true of poetry in Stalin's regime, and was in this country during the McCarthy period. This "creative tranquility" and this "secret freedom" are precisely what the dogmatists cannot tolerate. Stanley Kunitz believes the poet is inevitably the adversary of the state. The poet, he says, is a witness to the possibility of revelation. This the politically rigid cannot stand.

Dogmatists of all kinds—scientific, economic, moral, as well as political—are threatened by the creative freedom of the artist. This is necessarily and inevitably so. We cannot escape our anxiety over the fact that the artists together with creative persons of all sorts, are the possible destroyers of our nicely ordered systems. For the creative impulse is the speaking of the voice and the expressing of the forms of the preconscious and unconscious; and this is, by its very nature, a threat to rationality and external control. The dogmatists then try to take over the artist. The church, in certain periods, harnessed him to prescribed subjects and methods. Capitalism tries to take over the artist by buying him. And Soviet realism tried to do so by social proscription. The result, by the very nature of the creative impulse, is fatal to art. If it were possible to control the artist—and I do not believe it is—it would mean the death of art.

FOUR

◘

CREATIVITY AND
ENCOUNTER

I WISH TO PROPOSE a theory and to make some remarks about it, arising largely out of my contacts and discussions with artists and poets. The theory is: *Creativity occurs in an act of encounter and is to be understood with this encounter as its center.*

Cézanne sees a tree. He sees it in a way no one else has ever seen it. He experiences, as he no doubt would have said, "being grasped by the tree." The arching grandeur of the tree, the mothering spread, the delicate balance as the tree grips the earth—all these and many more characteristics of the tree are absorbed into his perception and are felt throughout his nervous structure. These are part of the vision he experiences. This vision involves an omission of some aspects of the scene and a greater emphasis on other aspects and the ensuing rearrangement of the whole; but it is more than the sum of all these. Primarily it is a vision that is now not tree, but Tree; the concrete tree Cézanne looked at is formed into the essence of tree. However original and unrepeatable his vision is, it is still a vision of all trees triggered by his encounter with this particular one.

The painting that issues out of this encounter between a human being, Cézanne, and an objective reality, the tree, is literally new, unique and original. Something is born, comes into being, something that did not exist before—which is as good a definition of creativity as we can get. Thereafter everyone who looks at the painting with intensity of awareness and lets it speak to him or her will see the tree with the unique powerful movement, the intimacy between the tree and the landscape, and the architectural beauty which literally did not exist in our relation with trees until Cézanne experienced and painted them. I can say without exaggeration that I never really *saw* a tree until I had seen and absorbed Cézanne's paintings of them.

1

The very fact that the creative act is such an encounter between two poles is what makes it so hard to study. It is easy enough to find the subjective pole, the person, but it is much harder to define the objective pole, the "world" or "reality." Since my emphasis here is on the encounter itself, I shall not worry too much at the moment about such definitions. In his book *Poetry and Experience*, Archibald MacLeish uses the most universal terms possible for the two poles of the encounter: "Being and Non-being." He quotes a Chinese poet: "We poets struggle with Non-being to force it to yield Being. We knock upon silence for an answering music."[1]

"Consider what this means," MacLeish ruminates. "The 'Being' which the poem is to contain derives from 'Non-being,' not from the poet. And the 'music' which the poem is to own comes not from us who make the poem but from the silence; comes in *answer* to our knock. The verbs are eloquent: 'struggle,' 'force,' 'knock.' The poet's labor is to struggle with the meaninglessness and silence of the world until he can force it to mean; until he can make the silence answer and the Non-being be. It is a labor which undertakes to 'know' the world not by exegesis or demonstration or proofs but directly, as a man knows apple in the mouth."[2] This is a beautifully expressed antidote to our common assumption that the subjective projection is *all* that occurs in the creative act, and a reminder of the inescapable mystery that surrounds the creative process.

The vision of the artist or the poet is the intermediate determinant between the subject (the person) and the objective pole (the world-waiting-to-be). It will be non-being until the poet's struggle brings forth an answering meaning. The greatness of a poem or a painting is not that it portrays the *thing* observed or experienced, but that it portrays the artist's or the poet's vision cued off by his encounter with the reality. Hence the poem or the painting is unique, original, never to be duplicated. No matter how many times Monet returned to paint the cathedral at Rouen, each canvas was a new painting expressing a new vision.

Here we must guard against one of the most serious errors in the psychoanalytic interpretation of creativity. This is the attempt to find something within the individual which is then projected onto the work of art, or some early experience which is transferred to the canvas or written into the poem. Obviously, early experiences play exceedingly important roles in determining how artists will encounter their world.

But these subjective data can never explain the encounter itself.

Even in the cases of abstract artists, where the process of painting seems most subjective, the relationship between being and non-being is certainly present and may be sparked by the artist's encountering the brilliant colors on the palette or the inviting rough whiteness of the canvas. Painters have described the excitement of this moment: it seems like a re-enactment of the creation story, with being suddenly becoming alive and possessing a vitality of its own. Mark Tobey fills his canvases with elliptical, calligraphic lines, beautiful whirls that seem at first glance to be completely abstract and to come from nowhere at all except his own subjective musing. But I shall never forget how struck I was, on visiting Tobey's studio one day, to see strewn around books on astronomy and photographs of the Milky Way. I knew then that Tobey experiences the movement of the stars and solar constellations as the external pole of his encounter.

The receptivity of the artist must never be confused with passivity. Receptivity is the artist's holding him- or herself alive and open to hear what being may speak. Such receptivity requires a nimbleness, a fine-honed sensitivity in order to let one's self be the vehicle of whatever vision may emerge. It is the opposite of the authoritarian demands impelled by "will power." I am quite aware of all the jokes that appear in *The New Yorker* and elsewhere showing the artist sitting disconsolately in front of the easel, brush in passive hand, waiting for the inspiration to come. But an artist's "waiting," funny as it may look in cartoons, is not to be confused with laziness or passivity. It requires a high degree of attention, as when a diver is poised on the end of the springboard, not jumping but holding his or her muscles in sensitive balance for the right second. It is an active listening, keyed to hear the answer, alert to see whatever can be glimpsed when the vision or the words do come. It is a waiting for the birthing process to begin to move in its own organic time. It is necessary that the artist have this sense of timing, that he or she respect these periods of receptivity as part of the mystery of creativity and creation.

2

A remarkable example of the creative encounter is given in the small book written by James Lord in recounting his experience of posing for Alberto Giacometti. Having been friends for some time, these two men could be entirely open with each other. Lord often made notes directly after the posing session of what Giacometti had said and done, and out of them he has put together this valuable monograph about the experience of encounter that occurs in creativity.

He reveals, first, the great degree of anxiety and agony that the encounter generated in Giacometti. When Lord would arrive at the studio for his sitting, Giacometti would often disconsolately occupy himself half an hour or more doings odds and ends with his sculpture, literally afraid to start on the painting. When he did bring himself to get into the painting, the anxiety became overt. At one point, writes Lord, Giacometti started gasping and stamping his foot:

"Your head is going away!" he exclaimed. "It's going away completely!"

"It will come back again," I said.

He shook his head. "Not necessarily. Maybe the canvas will become completely empty. And then what will become of me? I'll die of it!" . . .

He reached into his pocket, pulled out his handkerchief, stared at it for a moment, as though he didn't know what it was, then with a moan threw it onto the floor. Suddenly he shouted very loudly, "I shriek! I scream!"[3]

Lord goes on at another point:

To talk to his model while he is working distracts him, I think, from the constant anxiety which is a result of his conviction that he cannot hope to represent on the canvas what he sees before him. This anxiety often bursts forth in the form of melancholy gasps, furious expletives, and occasional loud cries of rage and/or distress. He suffers. There is no doubt about it. . . .

Giacometti is committed to his work in a particularly intense and total way. The creative compulsion is never wholly absent from him, never leaves him a moment of complete peace.[4]

So intense is the encounter that he often identifies the painting on the easel with the actual flesh-and-blood person posing. One day his foot accidentally struck the catch that holds the easel shelf at the proper level, which caused the canvas to fall abruptly for a foot or two.

"Oh, excuse me!" he said. I laughed and observed that he'd excused himself as though he'd caused me to fall instead of the painting. "That's exactly what I did feel," he answered.[5]

In Giacometti this anxiety was associated, as it was in his revered Cézanne, with a great deal of self-doubt.

In order to go on, to hope, to believe that there is some chance of his actually creating what he ideally visualizes, he is obliged to feel that it is necessary to start his entire career over again every day, as it were, from scratch. . . . he often feels that the particular sculpture or painting on which he happens to be working at the moment is that one which will for the very first time express what he subjectively experiences in response to an objective reality.[6]

Lord correctly assumes that the anxiety is related to the gap between the ideal vision that the artist is trying to paint and the objective results. Here he discusses the contradiction that every artist experiences:

This fundamental contradiction, arising from the hopeless discrepancy between conception and realization, is at the root of all artistic creation, and it helps explain the anguish which seems to be an unavoidable component of that experience. Even as "happy" an artist as Renoir was not immune to it.[7]

What meant something, what alone existed with a life of its own was his [Giacometti's] indefatigable, interminable struggle via the act of painting to express in visual terms a perception of reality that had happened to coincide momentarily with my head [which Giacometti was then trying to paint]. To achieve this was of course impossible, because what is essentially abstract can never be made concrete without altering its essence. But he was committed, he was, in fact *condemned* to the attempt, which at times seemed rather like the task of Sisyphus.[8]

One day Lord happened to see Giacometti in a café.

And, indeed, miserable was what he did seem to be. This, I thought, was the true Giacometti, sitting alone at the back of a café, oblivious to the admiration and recognition of the world, staring into a void from which no solace could come, tormented by the hopeless dichotomy of his ideal yet *condemned by that helplessness to struggle as long as he lived to try to overcome it.* What consolation was it that the newspapers of many countries spoke of him, that museums everywhere exhibited his work, that people he would never know knew and admired him. None. None at all.[9]

When we see the intimate feelings and inner experiences of an eminent artist like Giacometti, we smile at the absurd talk in some psychotherapeutic circles of "adjusting" people, making people "happy," or training out of them by simple behavior modification techniques all pain and grief and conflict and anxiety. How hard for humankind to absorb the deeper meaning of the myth of Sisyphus!—to see that "success" and "applause" are the bitch goddesses we always secretly knew they were. To see that the purpose of human existence in a man like Giacometti has nothing whatever to do with reassurance or conflict-free adjustment.

Giacometti was rather devoted—"condemned," to use Lord's fitting term—to the struggle to perceive and reproduce the world around him through his own vision of being human. He knew there was no other alternative for him. This challenge gave his life meaning. He and his kind seek to bring their own visions of what it means to be human, and to see through that vision to a world of reality, however ephemeral, however consistently that reality vanishes each time you concentrate on it. How absurd are the rationalistic assumptions that all one has to do is to remove from the world its curtains of superstition and ignorance and there suddenly will be reality, pristine and pure!

Giacometti sought to see reality through his ideal vision. He sought to find the *ground forms*, the basic structure of reality, below the strewn surface of the arena where bitch goddesses cavort. He could not escape devoting himself unstintingly to the question: *Is there some place where reality speaks our language, where it answers us if we but understand the hieroglyphics?* He knew the rest of us would be no more successful than he was in finding the answer; but we have his contribution to work with, and thus we are helped.

3

Out of the encounter is born the work of art. This is true not only of painting, but of poetry and other forms of creativity. W. H. Auden once remarked to me in private conversation: "The poet marries the language, and out of this marriage the poem is born." How *active* this makes language in the creation of a poem! It is not that language is merely a tool of communication, or that we only use language to express our ideas; it is just as true that language uses *us*. Language is the symbolic repository of the meaningful experience of ourselves and our fellow human beings down through history, and, as such, it reaches out to grasp us in the creating of a poem. We must not forget that the original Greek and Hebrew words meaning "to know" meant also "to have sexual relations." One reads in the Bible "Abraham *knew* his wife and she conceived." The etymology of the term demonstrates the prototypical fact that knowledge itself—as well as poetry, art, and other creative products—arises out of the dynamic encounter between subjective and objective poles.

The sexual metaphor indeed expresses the importance of encounter. In sexual intercourse the two persons encounter each other; they withdraw partially to unite with each other again, experiencing every nuance of knowing, not knowing, in order to know each other again. The man becomes united with the woman and the woman with the man, and the partial withdrawal can be seen as the expedient by which both have the ecstatic experience of being filled again. Each is active and passive in his and her way. It is a demonstration that the *process* of knowing is what is important; if the male simply rests within the woman, nothing will happen beyond the prolonging of the wonder of the intimacy. It is the continuous experiencing of encounter and re-encounter that is the significant happening from the viewpoint of ultimate creativity. Sexual intercourse is the ultimate intimacy of two beings in the fullest and richest encounter possible. It is highly significant that this is the experience that is also the highest form of creativity in the respect that it can produce a new being.

The particular forms the offspring take in poems, drama, and the plastic arts are *symbols* and *myths*. Symbols (like Cézanne's tree) or myths (like that of Oedipus) express the relationship between conscious and unconscious experience, between one's individual present existence and human history. Symbol and myth are the living, immediate forms that emerge from encounter, and they consist of the dialectic interrelationship—the living, active, continuous mutual influence in which any change in one is bound to bring a change in the other—of subjective and objective poles. They are born out of the heightened consciousness of the encounter we are describing; and they have their power to grasp us because they require from us and give us an experience of heightened consciousness.

Thus in the history of culture artistic discovery precedes other forms. As Sir Herbert Read puts it, "On the basis of this [artistic] activity, a 'symbolic discourse' becomes possible, and religion, philosophy and science follow as consequent modes of thought." This is not to say that reason is the more civilized form and art the more *primitive* one, in a pejorative sense—an egregious error unfortunately often found in our rationalistic Western culture. This is, rather, to say that the creative encounter in the art form is "total"—it expresses a wholeness of experience; and science and philosophy abstract partial aspects for their subsequent study.

4

One distinguishing characteristic of the encounter is the degree of *intensity*, or what I would call *passion*. I am not referring here to the *quantity* of emotion. I mean a *quality* of commitment, which may be present in little experiences—such as a brief glance out the window at a tree—that do not necessarily involve any great quantity of emotion. But these temporally brief experiences may have a considerable significance for the sensitive person, here viewed as the person with a capacity for passion. Hans Hofmann, venerable dean of abstract painters in this country and one of our most expert and experienced teachers, remarked that art students these days have a great deal of talent but that they lack passion or commitment. Hofmann went on to say, interestingly enough, that his men students get married early for reasons of security and become dependent on their wives, and that often it is only through their wives that he, as their teacher, can draw out their talent. The fact that talent is plentiful but passion is lacking seems to me to be a fundamental facet of the problem of creativity in many fields today, and our ways of approaching creativity by evading the encounter have played directly into this trend. We worship technique—talent—as a way of evading the anxiety of the direct encounter.

Kierkegaard understood this so well! "The present writer . . ." he wrote about himself, "can easily foresee his fate in an age when passion has been obliterated in favor of learning, in an age when an author who wants to have readers must take care to write in such a way that the book can easily be perused during the afternoon nap."

5

At this point we see the inadequacy of the concept commonly used in psychoanalytic circles to explain creativity—"regression in the service of the ego." In my own endeavors to understand creative people in psychoanalysis and to understand the creative act in general, I find this theory unsatisfactory. This is not only because of its negative character, but chiefly because it proposes a partial solution that diverts us from the center of the creative act and therefore away from any full understanding of creativity.

In supporting the theory of "regression in the service of the ego," Ernest Kris cites the work of the minor poet A. E. Housman, who, in his autobiography, describes his way of writing poetry as follows. After a full morning of teaching classes in Latin at Oxford, Housman would have lunch, with which he would drink a pint of beer, and would then take a walk. And in this somnambulistic mood, his poems would come to him. Kris, in line with this theory, correlates *passiveness and receptivity* with creativity. It is true that most of us find an appeal in such lines of Housman:

> Be still, my soul, be still;
> the arms you bear are brittle ...

And the appeal does call forth a nostalgic, regressive mood in us as readers as well as, ostensibly, in Housman himself.

I grant, thus, that creativity often *seems* to be a regressive phenomenon, and does bring out archaic, infantile, unconscious psychic contents in the artist. But is this not parallel to what Poincaré points out (see Chapter Three, pp. 67–75) when he discusses how his insights come in periods of rest after his great labors? He specifically cautions us *not* to assume that it is the rest that produces the creativity. The rest—or regression—only serves to release the person from his or her intense efforts and the accompanying inhibitions, so that the creative impulse can have free rein to express itself. When the archaic elements in a poem or a picture have genuine power to move others, and when they have a universality of meaning—that is, when they are genuine symbols—it is because some encounter is occurring on a more basic, comprehensive level.

If, however, we take as a contrast some lines from one of the major poets of our day, William Butler Yeats, we find a quite different mood. In "The Second Coming," Yeats describes modern man's condition:

> Things fall apart; the center cannot hold;
> Mere anarchy is loosed upon the world . . .

He then tells us what he sees:

> The Second Coming! Hardly are those words out
> When a vast image . . .
> Troubles my sight; somewhere in sands of the desert
> A shape with lion body and the head of a man,
> A gaze blank and pitiless as the sun,
> Is moving its slow thighs . . .
> And what rough beast, its hour come round at last,
> Slouches towards Bethlehem to be born?

What tremendous power in this last symbol! It is a new revelation, with beauty but with terrible meaning in relation to the situation in which we modern human beings find ourselves. The reason Yeats has such power is that he writes out of an intensity of consciousness that includes archaic elements because they are part of him, as they are of every person, and will emerge in any intensely aware moment. But the symbol has its power precisely from the fact that it is an encounter that also includes the most dedicated and passionate intellectual effort. In writing this poem Yeats was *receptive*, but by no stretch of the imagination passive. "The poet's labor," MacLeish tells us, is "not to wait until the cry gathers of itself in his own throat."[10]

Obviously, poetic and creative insights of all sorts come to us in moments of relaxation. They come not haphazardly, however, but come only in those areas in which we are intensively committed and on which we concentrate in our waking, conscious experience. It may be, as we have said, that the insights can break through only in moments of relaxation; but to say this is to describe *how* they come rather than to explain their genesis. My poet friends tell me that if you want to write poetry, or even read it, the hour after a full lunch and a pint of beer is just the time *not* to pick. Choose rather the moments in which you are capable of your highest, most intense consciousness. If you write poetry during your afternoon nap, it will be perused that way.

The issue here is not simply which poets you happen to like. It is much more basic—namely, the nature of the symbols and myths that are born in the creative act. Symbol and myth do bring into awareness infantile, archaic dreads, unconscious longings, and similar primitive psychic content. This is their *regressive* aspect. But they also bring out new meaning, new forms, and disclose a reality that was literally not present before, a reality that is not merely subjective but has a second pole which is outside ourselves. This is the *progressive* side of symbol and myth. This aspect points ahead. It is integrative. It is a progressive revealing of structure in our relation to nature and our own existence, as the French philosopher Paul Ricoeur so well states. It is a road to universals beyond discrete personal experience. It is this *progressive* aspect of symbols and myths that is almost completely omitted in the traditional Freudian psychoanalytic approach.

This heightened consciousness, which we have identified as characteristic of the encounter, the state in which the dichotomy between subjective experience and objective reality is overcome and symbols which reveal new meaning are born, is historically termed *ecstasy*. Like passion, ecstasy is a quality of emotion (or, more accurately, a quality of relationship one side of which is emotional) rather than a quantity. Ecstasy is a temporary transcending of the subject-object dichotomy. It is interesting that in psychology we dodge that problem, Maslow's work on the peak experience being a notable exception. Or, when we do speak of ecstasy we are implicitly pejorative or assume that it is neurotic.

The experience of encounter also brings with it *anxiety*. I need not remind you, after our discussion of Giacometti's experience, of the "fear and trembling" of artists and creative people in their moments of creative encounter. The myth of Prometheus is the classical expression of this anxiety. W. H. Auden once remarked that he always experiences anxiety when he writes poetry except when he is "playing." *Playing* may be defined as encounter in which anxiety is temporarily bracketed. But in mature creativity, anxiety must be confronted if the artist (and the rest of us who benefit from his work later on) is to experience the joy in the creative work.

I am impressed by Frank Barron's studies of creative persons in art and science,[11] for he shows them directly confronting their anxiety. Barron designated his "creative persons" as those who were recognized by their peers as having made distinguished contributions to their field. He showed them as well as a control group of "normal" people a series of Rorschachlike cards, some of which had orderly, systematic designs on them and others disorderly, unsymmetrical, and chaotic designs. The "normal" people selected the orderly, symmetrical cards as the designs they liked the most—they liked their universe to be "in shape." But the creative persons selected the chaotic, disorderly cards—they found these more challenging and interesting. They could be like God in the Book of Genesis, creating order out of chaos. They chose the "broken" universe; they got joy out of encountering it and forming it into order. They could accept the anxiety and use it in molding their disorderly universe "closer to the heart's desire."

According to the theory proposed here, anxiety is understandably a concomitant of the shaking of the self-world relationship that occurs in the encounter. Our sense of identity is threatened; the world is not as we experienced it before, and since self and world are always correlated, *we* no longer are what we were before. Past, present, and future form a new Gestalt. Obviously this is only rarely true in a complete sense (Gauguin going to the South Sea Islands, or Van Gogh becoming psychotic), but it is true that the creative encounter does change to some degree the self-world relationship. The anxiety we feel is temporary rootlessness, disorientation; it is the anxiety of nothingness.

Creative people, as I see them, are distinguished by the fact that they can live with anxiety, even though a high price may be paid in terms of insecurity, sensitivity, and defenselessness for the gift of the "divine madness," to borrow the term used by the classical Greeks. They do not run away from non-being, but by encountering and wrestling with it, force it to produce being. They knock on silence for an answering music; they pursue meaninglessness. until they can force it to mean.*

---

* Since I have come out in support of meditation earlier (Chapter One), I feel it necessary to state my disagreement with a claim of one kind of relaxation, namely transcendental meditation, that it is the "science of creative intelligence" and stimulates creative thinking. True, it does further one aspect of creativity—namely spontaneity, intuitively "feeling one's self into the universe," and similar things associated with the "comfort" Maharishi talks about so often. These are the aspects of creativity associated with children's play. But TM completely omits the element of encounter which is essential for mature creativity. The aspects of struggle, of tension, of constructive stress—the emotions that Giacometti was experiencing in Lord's account—are forgotten in TM.

I have discussed this matter with Frank Barron, psychologist at the University of California at Santa Cruz and, in my judgment, the foremost authority on the psychology of creativity in this country. Barron, like myself, has addressed regional conferences of TM. The card test mentioned above has been given to some groups of transcendental meditators. The results (not yet published) were negative—that is, the meditators tended to choose the cards with orderly and symmetrical forms. This is the opposite to Barron's results with especially creative persons. Also Gary Swartz studied teachers of transcendental meditation and found that on tests of creativity they scored worse or only as well as control groups. (See *Psychology Today*, July, 1975, p. 50).

When I am engaged in writing something important to me, I find that if I engage in the customary twenty-minute meditation period before writing, my universe has become too straightened out, too orderly. Then I have nothing to write about. My encounter has vanished into thin air. My "problems" are all solved. I feel bliss, to be sure, but I cannot write.

I prefer, therefore, to endure the chaos, to face "complexity and perplexity," as Barron puts it. Then I am impelled by this chaos to seek order, to struggle with it until I can find a deeper, underlying form. I believe I am then engaged in what MacLeish describes as struggling with the meaninglessness and silence of the world until I can force it to mean, until I can make the silence answer and the non-being be.

After the morning's period of writing, I can then use meditation for its authentic purpose—namely a deep relaxation of mind and body.

It is unfortunate for the movement—in that it presages a strong reaction against the movement sometime in the future—that its leaders are not more open to the limitations of TM and of Maharishi. All descriptions I have seen of TM blandly assume that Maharishi's gospel has no limitations at all. To those who wish a more complete picture, I recommend the article by Constance Holden, "Maharishi International University: 'Science of Creative Intelligence,'" *Science*, Vol. 187 (March 28, 1975), 1176.

FIVE

□

THE DELPHIC ORACLE
AS THERAPIST

IN THE MOUNTAINS at Delphi stands a shrine
that for many centuries was of great importance to ancient Greece. The Greeks had a genius
for locating their shrines in lovely places, but
Delphi is especially magnificent with a long val-
ley stretching between massive ranges on one
side and on the other the deep blue-green of the
Bay of Cornith. It is a place where one immediately feels the awe and the sense of grandeur
which befits the nature of the shrine. Here the
Greeks found help in meeting their anxiety. In
this temple, from the chaotic archaic age down

through classical times, Apollo gave counsel through his priestesses. Socrates was even to find there inscribed on the wall of the entrance hall to the temple his famous dictum "Know thyself," which has become the central touchstone for psychotherapy ever since.

The sensitive Greek, anxious about himself, his family, and his future in those upset times, could find guidance here, for Apollo knew the meaning of "the complicated games the gods play with humanity," writes Prof. E. R. Dodds. In his excellent study of the irrational in ancient Greek culture, he continues:

Without Delphi, Greek society could scarcely have endured the tensions to which it was subjected in the Archaic Age. The crushing sense of human ignorance and human insecurity, the dread of divine *phthonos*, the dread of *miasma*—the accumulated burden of these things would have been unendurable without the assurance which such an omniscient divine counsellor could give, the assurance that behind the seeming chaos there was knowledge and purpose.[1]

The anxiety that Apollo helped people meet was the apprehension that accompanies a formative, fermenting, creative, powerfully expanding period. It is important to see that it was not neurotic anxiety, characterized by withdrawal, inhibition, and the blocking off of vitality. The archaic period in ancient Greece was the time of emergence and vital growth fraught with distress that resulted from the chaos of expanding outer and inner limits. The Greeks were experiencing the anxiety of new possibilities—psychologically, politically, aesthetically, and spiritually. These new possibilities, and the anxiety that always accompanies such challenges, were forced upon them whether they wished it or not.

The shrine at Delphi rose to prominence at a time when the old stability and order of the family were crumbling and the individual soon would have to be responsible for himself. In Homeric Greece, Odysseus' wife Penelope and son Telemachus could oversee the estate whether Odysseus was there or at the wars in Troy or tossed for ten years on the "wine-dark sea." But now, in the archaic period, families must be welded into cities. Each young Telemachus felt himself standing on the brink of the time when he would have to choose his own future and find his own place as part of a new city. How fertile the myth of the young Telemachus has been for modern writers who are searching for their own identity. James Joyce presents one aspect of it in *Ulysses.* Thomas Wolfe refers often to Telemachus as the myth of the search for the father, which was Wolfe's search as truly as it was the ancient Greek's. Wolfe, like any modern Telemachus, found that the hard, cold truth was "you can't go home again."

The city-states were struggling in anarchy, tyrant following tyrant (a term that in Greek does not have the usual destructive connotation it carries in English).[2] The upsurging leaders tried to weld the new power into some order. New forms of governing the city-states, new laws, and new interpretations of the gods were emerging, all of which gave the individual new psychological powers. In such a period of change and growth, *emergence* is often experienced by the individual as *emergency* with all its attendant stress.

Into this ferment came the symbol of Apollo and his shrine at Delphi and the rich myths on which they were based.

1

It is important to remember that Apollo is the god of *form*, the god of reason and logic. Thus it is no accident that his shrine became the important one in this chaotic time and that through this god of proportion and balance the citizens sought assurance that there was meaning and purpose behind the seeming chaos. Form and proportion and the golden mean were essential if these men and women were to control their deep passions, not in order to tame these passions but to turn to constructive use the daimonic powers that the Greeks knew so well in nature and in themselves. Apollo is also the god of art since form—elegance—is an essential characteristic of beauty. Indeed, Parnassus, the mountain at Delphi on whose flank Apollo's shrine stood, has become a symbol in all Western languages for devotion to the virtues of the mind.

We appreciate more of the rich meaning of such a myth when we note that Apollo is the god of light—not only the light of the sun, but the light of the mind, the light of reason, the light of insight. He is often called Helios, the word in Greek for "sun," and Phoebus Apollo, the god of brightness and radiance. Finally, we note the most cogent point of all: Apollo is the god of healing and well-being, and his son Asclepius is the god of medicine.

All of these attributes of Apollo, created as they were by collective unconscious processes in the mythology of the dark pre-Homeric centuries, are interwoven with fantastic literal as well as figurative significance. How consistent and meaningful it is that this is the god of good counsel, of psychological and spiritual insight, who will give guidance to a highly vital, formative age! An Athenian setting out on the trip to Delphi to consult Apollo would be turning over in his imagination at almost every moment in the journey this figure of the god of light and healing. Spinoza adjured us to fix our attention on a desired virtue, and we would thus tend to acquire it. Our Greek would be doing this on his trip, and the psychological processes of anticipation, hope, and faith would already be at work. Thus he would be proleptically participating in his own "cure." His conscious intentions and his deeper intentionality would be already committed to the event about to take place. For the one who participates in them, symbols and myths carry their own healing power.

This chapter is thus an essay on the *creating of one's self*. The self is made up, on its growing edge, of the models, forms, metaphors, myths, and all other kinds of psychic content which give it direction in its self-creation. This is a process that goes on continuously. As Kierkegaard well said, the self is only that which it is in the process of becoming. Despite the obvious determinism in human life—especially in the physical aspect of one's self in such simple things as color of eyes, height, relative length of life, and so on—there is also, clearly, this element of self-directing, self-forming. Thinking and self-creating are inseparable. When we become aware of all the fantasies in which we see ourselves in the future, pilot ourselves this way or that, this becomes obvious.

This continuous influencing of the direction of a person's development goes on in the ancient Greek or the modern American, deny it as we wish. Spinoza's counsel, mentioned above, is one way this piloting function can be actualized. The mass of myths dealing with the reincarnation of an individual into one or another life form, its status dependent on how this person has lived his or her life, attests to the awareness in the experience of the race that the individual does have some responsibility for how he or she lives. Sartre's argument that we invent ourselves by virtue of the multitude of our choices may be overstated, but its partial truth must nevertheless be admitted.

Human freedom involves our capacity to pause between stimulus and response and, in that pause, to choose the one response toward which we wish to throw our weight. The capacity to create ourselves, based upon this freedom, is inseparable from consciousness or self-awareness.

We are concerned here with how the oracle at Delphi furthers this process of self-creation. Clearly self-creating is actualized by our hopes, our ideals, our images, and all sorts of imagined constructs that we may hold from time to time in the forefront of our attention. These "models" function consciously as well as unconsciously; they are shown in fantasy as well as in overt behavior. The summary terms for this process are *symbols* and *myths*. And the shrine of Apollo at Delphi was a concrete expression of these symbols and myths, and it was where they were embodied in ritual.

2

We can see in the superb statues of Apollo carved at this time—the archaic figure with his strong, straight form, his calm beauty of head, his ordered features which are eloquent with controlled passion, even down to the slight "knowing" smile on the almost straight mouth—how this god could be the symbol in which the Greek artists as well as other citizens of that period perceived their longed-for order. There is a curious feature in these statues that I have seen: the eyes are *dilated,* made more open than is normal in the head of a living man or in classical Greek statues. If you walk through the archaic Greek room of the National Museum in Athens, you will be struck by the fact that the dilated eyes of the marble figures of Apollo give an expression of great alertness. What a contrast to the relaxed, almost sleepy eyes of the familiar fourth-century head of Hermes by Praxiteles.

These dilated eyes of the archaic Apollo are characteristic of apprehension. They express the anxiety—the excessive awareness, the "looking about" on all sides lest something unknown might happen—that goes with living in a fomenting age. There is a remarkable parallel between these eyes and the eyes in the figures Michelangelo painted in another formative period, the Renaissance. Almost all of Michelangelo's human beings, powerful and triumphant as they appear at first glance, have, on closer inspection, the dilated eyes which are a telltale sign of anxiety. And as if to demonstrate that he is expressing the inner tensions not only of his age but of himself as a member of his age, Michelangelo in his self-portraits paints eyes that are again markedly distended in the way that is typical of apprehension.

The poet Rilke also was struck by Apollo's prominent eyes with their quality of seeing deeply. In his "Archaic Torso of Apollo," he speaks of ". . . his legendary head in which the eyeballs ripened," and then continues,

                        . . . But
his torso still glows like a candelabrum
in which his gaze, only turned low,

holds and gleams. Else could not the curve
of the breast blind you, nor in the slight turn
of the loins could a smile be running
to that middle, which carried procreation.

Else would this stone be standing maimed and short
under the shoulders' translucent plunge
nor flimmering like the fell of beasts of prey

nor breaking out of all its contours
like a star: for there is no place
that does not see you. You must change your life.[3]

In this vivid picture we note how well Rilke catches the essence of *controlled passion*—not inhibited or repressed passion, as was to be the goal during the later Hellenistic age of the Greek teachers who had become afraid of vital drives. What a far cry is Rilke's interpretation from Victorian inhibition and repression of drives. These early Greeks, who wept and made love and killed with zest, gloried in passion and Eros and the daimonic. (Persons in therapy nowadays, considering the strange spectacle in ancient Greece, remark on the fact that it is the *strong* person like Odysseus or Achilles who weeps.) But the Greeks knew also that these drives had to be directed and controlled. It was the essence, they believed, of a man of virtue (*arete*) that he choose his passions rather than be chosen by them. In this lies the explanation of why they did not need to go through the self-castrating practice of denying Eros and the daimonic, as modern man does.

The sense of the archaic period is shown even in Rilke's curious last sentence, which seems at first (but only at first) to be a *non sequitur*: "You must change your life." This is the call of passionate beauty, the demand that beauty makes on us by its very presence that we also participate in the new form. Not at all moralistic (the call has nothing whatever to do with right or wrong), it is nevertheless an imperious demand which grasps us with the insistence that we take into our own lives this new harmonious form.

3

How the oracle of Apollo functioned and where the advice it gave came from are, of course, fascinating questions. But unfortunately little seems to be known on this subject. The shrine was veiled in secrecy; those who directed it could not only give counsel to others but could also keep their own. Plato tells us that a "prophetic madness" overcame the Pythia, the priestess who served in the temple as mouthpiece for Apollo. From this "madness" there emerged some "creative insight," so Plato believed, which represented deeper-than-normal levels of consciousness. "It is to their madness," he writes in his *Phaedrus*, "that we owe the many benefits that the Pythia of Delphi and the priestesses of Dodona were able to bestow upon Greece both privately and in public life, for when they were in their right minds their achievements amounted to little or nothing." [4] This is a clear statement of one side of a controversy that has raged through human history about the source of inspiration—to what extent does creativity come from madness?

Apollo spoke in the first person through the Pythia. Her voice changed and became husky, throaty, and quavering like that of a modern medium. The god was said to enter her at the very moment of her seizure, or *enthusiasm*, as the root of that term, *en-theo* ("in god"), literally suggests.

Before the "seance" the priestess went through several ritualistic acts, such as special bathing and perhaps drinking from a sacred spring, presumedly with the customary autosuggestive effects. But the oft-repeated statement that she breathed vapors issuing from a fissure in the rocks of the shrine which induced a hypnotic effect is disposed of summarily by Professor Dodds:

As for the famous "vapours" to which the Pythia's inspiration was once confidently ascribed, they are a Hellenistic invention. . . . Plutarch, who knew the facts, saw the difficulties of the vapour theory, and seems finally to have rejected it altogether; but like the Stoic philosophers, nineteenth-century scholars seized with relief on a nice solid materialist explanation.[5]

Dodds goes on to remark pithily that "less has been heard of this theory since the French excavations showed that there are to-day no vapours, and no 'chasm' from which vapours could once have come."[6] Obviously such explanations are needless in view of the present-day evidence of anthropology and abnormal psychology.

The Pythian priestesses themselves seemed to be simple, uneducated women (Plutarch tells of one who was the daughter of a peasant). But modern scholars have a high respect for the intelligence system of the oracle. The decisions of Delphi showed sufficient signs of a consistent policy to convince scholars that human intelligence, intuition, and insight did play a decisive role in the process. Although Apollo committed some notorious blunders in his predictions and advice, especially during the Persian wars, the Greeks, with an attitude like many people in psychotherapy have toward their therapist today, forgave him evidently because of the useful advice and help he had given at other times.

The point that interests us most is the function of the shrine as a communal symbol that had the power to draw out the preconscious and unconscious collective insights of the Greeks. Delphi's communal, collective aspect had a sound foundation: the shrine was originally devoted to the earth goddesses before being dedicated to Apollo. Also it is collective in the sense that Dionysus, Apollo's opposite, was also a strong influence at Delphi. Greek vases show Apollo, presumably at Delphi, grasping Dionysus's hand. Plutarch does not exaggerate much when he writes, "as regards the Delphic oracle the part played by Dionysus was no less than Apollo's." [7]

Any genuine symbol, with its accompanying

ceremonial rite, becomes the mirror that reflects insights, new possibilities, new wisdom, and other psychological and spiritual phenomena that we do not dare experience on our own. We cannot for two reasons. The first is our own anxiety: the new insights often—and, we could even say, typically—would frighten us too much were we to take full and lonely responsibility for them. In an age of ferment such insights may come frequently, and they require more psychological and spiritual responsibility than most individuals are prepared to bear. In dreams people can let themselves do things—such as killing their parent or their child, or thinking "my mother hated me," for instance—that would normally be too horrible to think or say in ordinary speech. We hesitate to think these and similar things even in daydreams since such fantasies are felt to carry more individual responsibility than night dreams. But if we can have a dream say it, or have Apollo through his oracle say it, we can be much more frank about our new truth.

The second reason is we escape hubris. Socrates could assert that Apollo at Delphi had pronounced him the wisest man then living, a claim —whether it be Socratic wit or not—he could never have made on his own.

How did one interpret the counsel of the priestesses? This is the same as asking: How does one interpret a symbol? The divinations of the priestess were generally couched in poetry and often were uttered "in wild, onomatopoeic cries as well as articulate speech, and this 'raw material' certainly had to be interpreted and worked over." [8] Like mediumistic statements of all ages, these were sufficiently cryptic not only to leave the way open for interpretation, but to *require* it. And often they were susceptible to two or many different interpretations.

The process was like the interpretation of a dream. Harry Stack Sullivan used to teach young analysts-in-training not to interpret a dream as if it were the law of the Medes and the Persians, but to suggest two different meanings to the person being analyzed, thus requiring him or her to choose between them. The value of dreams, like these divinations, is not that they give a specific answer, but that they open up new areas of psychic reality, shake us out of our customary ruts, and throw light on a new segment of our lives. Thus the sayings of the shrine, like dreams, were not to be received passively; *the recipients had to "live" themselves into the message.*

During the Persian wars, for example, when the anxious Athenians had petitioned Apollo to give them guidance, word came from the oracle adjuring them to trust in "the wooden wall." The meaning of this enigma was hotly debated. As Herodotus tells the story, "Certain of the old men were of opinion that the god meant to tell them the acropolis would escape, for this was anciently defended by a wooden palisade. Others maintained that the god referred to wooden ships, which had best be at once got ready." Thereupon another part of the oracle caused debate, for some thought they should sail away without a fight and establish themselves in a new land. But Themistocles convinced the people that they were intended to engage in a sea fight near Salamis, which they did, destroying Xerxes' fleet in one of the decisive battles of history.[9]

Whatever the intention of the Delphic priests, the effect of ambiguous prophecies was to force the suppliants to think out their situation anew, to reconsider their plans, and to conceive of new possibilities.

Apollo, indeed, was nicknamed the "ambiguous one." Lest some budding therapists take this as an excuse for their own ambiguity, let us here note a difference between modern therapy and the divinations of the oracle. The utterances of the priestess are on a level closer to the recipients' unconscious, closer to *actual* dreams, in contrast to the interpretation of dreams in a therapeutic hour. Apollo speaks from deeper dimensions of consciousness in the citizen and the collective group (i.e., the city). Thus there can be a creative ambiguity, which occurs both in the original saying (or dream) and in the citizen's (or patient's) interpretation of it. The oracle has an advantage over the contemporary therapist. In any case, I believe a therapist ought to be as succinct as possible, and leave the inescapable ambiguity to the patient!

The counsels of Delphi were not advice in the strict sense, but rather were stimulants to the individual and to the group to look inward, to consult their own intuition and wisdom. The oracles put the problem in a new context so that it could be seen in a different way, a way in which new and as yet unimagined possibilities would become evident. It is a common misconception that such shrines, as well as modern therapy, tend to make the individual more passive. This would be bad therapy and a misinterpretation of the oracles. Both should do exactly the opposite; they should require individuals to recognize their own possibilities, enlightening new aspects of themselves and their interpersonal relationships. This process taps the source of creativity in people. It turns them inward toward their own creative springs.

In the *Apologia*, Socrates tells us how he tried to puzzle out what the god meant by telling his friend Chaerephon that no one in the world was wiser than he (Socrates). The philosopher came to the conclusion that it meant he was wisest because he admitted his own ignorance. The god also counseled Socrates to "know thyself." Ever since that time, thoughtful men like Nietzsche and Kierkegaard have been trying to fathom the meaning of the god's advice, and we are still stimulated to find new meanings in it. Nietzsche even interprets it as meaning just the opposite to what one would conclude at first glance: "What did the god mean who proclaimed 'Know thyself' to Socrates? Did he perchance mean, 'Cease to be concerned about thyself,' 'Be objective'?" Like the true symbols and/or myths they are, these utterances of the god yield unending richness as new and interesting meanings are unfolded.

4

There is another reason why an oracle can be significant as the embodiment of the unconscious collective insights of the group. A symbol or myth acts like a projective screen in drawing out the insight. Like Rorschach cards or Murray's Thematic Apperception Test, the oracle and its ceremonies are a screen that stimulates wonder and calls imagination into action.

But I must hasten to insert a caution. The process going on at such a place and time may be called "projection," but we must insist that it is not "projection" in any pejorative sense of the word, either in the psychoanalytical one in which an individual "projects" what is "sick" and therefore what he or she cannot face, nor in the empirical psychological sense in which it is implied that the process is simply subjective and that the cards or TAT pictures have nothing to do with the result. In my judgment, both of these pejorative uses of *projection* result from the common failure of Western man to understand the nature of symbol and myth.

The "screen" is not merely a blank mirror. It is, rather, *the objective pole necessary for calling forth the subjective processes of consciousness.* The Rorschach cards *are* definite and real forms of black and color, even though no one ever before has "seen" in them the things you or I may see in them. Such "projection" is in no sense a "regression" by definition or something less respectable than being able to say what you want to say in rational sentences without the cards. It is rather a legitimate and healthy exercise of imagination.

This process goes on all the time in art. Paint and canvas are objective things that have powerful and existential influences on the artist in bringing out his or her ideas and visions. Indeed, the artist is in a dialectical relation not only with paint and canvas, but with the shapes he or she sees in nature. The poet and the musician are in a similar relationship with their inherited language and musical notes. The artist, the poet, and the musician dare to bring forth new forms, new kinds of vitality and meaning. They are, at least partially, protected from "going crazy" in this process of radical emergence by the form given by the media—namely the paints, the marble, the words, the musical notes.

The shrine of Apollo at Delphi thus can most felicitously be seen as a communal symbol. We can postulate, then, that its insights come by a communal symbolic process involving both subjective factors in a dialectical relation with each other. For anyone who authentically uses the oracle, new forms, new ideal possibilities, new ethical and religious structures may be born from levels of experience that underlie and transcend the individual's customary waking consciousness. We have noted that Plato calls this process the ecstasy of "prophetic madness." Ecstasy is a time-honored method of transcending our ordinary consciousness and a way of helping us arrive at insights we could not attain otherwise. An element of ecstasy, however slight, is part and parcel of every genuine symbol and myth; for if we genuinely participate in the symbol or myth, we are for that moment taken "out of" and "beyond" ourselves.

The psychological approach to symbol and myth is only one of several possible avenues. In taking this approach I do not wish to "psychologize away" the myth's religious meaning. From this religious aspect of myth we get the insight (revelation) that comes from dialectical interplay of the subjective elements in the individual and the objective fact of the oracle. To the genuine believer, the myth is never purely psychological. It always includes an element of revelation, whether from the Greek Apollo, or the Hebrew Elohim, or the Oriental "Being." If we completely psychologized away this religious element, we would be unable to appreciate the power with which Aeschylus and Sophocles wrote their dramas and even unable to understand what they are talking about. Aeschylus and Sophocles and the other dramatists could write great tragedies because of the religious dimensions of the myths, which gave a structural undergirding to their belief in the dignity of the race and the meaning of its destiny.

SIX

□

ON THE LIMITS
OF CREATIVITY

O N A SATURDAY evening at an Esalen week end
in New York recently, a panel discussion on
the human prospect was held. The panel consisted of such insightful and stimulating persons
as Joyce Carol Oates, Gregory Bateson, and
William Irwin Thompson. The audience was
made up of seven or eight hundred eager individuals, expectantly set for an interesting discussion at the very least. In his opening remarks, the
chairman emphasized the theme that "the possibilities of the human being are unlimited."

But strange to say, there seemed, as the meeting went on, to be no problems to discuss. The vast vacuum filling the room was felt by both the panel and the audience alike. All the exciting issues that the participants on the panel had approached so eagerly had mysteriously vanished. As the discussion limped along to the end of an almost fruitless evening, the common question seemed to be: What had gone wrong?

I propose that the statement, "human possibilities are unlimited" is de-energizing. If you take it at face value, there is no real problem anymore. You can only stand up and sing hallelujah and then go home. Every problem will sooner or later be overcome by these unlimited possibilities; there remain only temporary difficulties that will go away of their own accord when the time comes. Contrary to the chairman's intention, statements like his actually terrorize the listener: it is like putting someone into a canoe and pushing him out into the Atlantic toward England with the cheery comment, "The sky's the limit." The canoer is only too aware of the fact that an inescapable real limit is also the bottom of the ocean.

In these notes I shall explore the hypothesis that limits are not only unavoidable in human life, they are also valuable. I shall also discuss the phenomenon that *creativity itself requires limits,* for the creative act arises out of the struggle of human beings with and against that which limits them.

To begin with, there is the inescapable physical limitation of death. We can postpone our death slightly, but nevertheless each of us will die and at some future time unknown to and unpredictable by us. Sickness is another limit. When we overwork we get ill in one form or another. There are obvious neurological limits. If the blood stops flowing to the brain for as little as a couple of minutes, a stroke or some other kind of serious damage occurs. Despite the fact that we can improve our intelligence to some degree, it remains radically limited by our physical and emotional environment.

There are also metaphysical limitations which are even more interesting. Each of us was born into a certain family in a certain country at a certain historical moment, all with no choice on our part. If we try to deny these facts—like Jay Gatsby in Fitzgerald's *The Great Gatsby*—we blind ourselves to reality and come to grief. True, we can surpass to some extent the limitations of our family backgrounds or our historical situation, but such transcendence can occur only to those who accept the fact of their limitation to begin with.

1. THE VALUE OF LIMITS

Consciousness itself is born out of the awareness of these limits. Human consciousness is the distinguishing feature of our existence; without limitations we would never have developed it. Consciousness is the awareness that emerges out of the dialectical tension between possibilities and limitations. Infants begin to be aware of limits when they experience the ball as different from themselves; mother is a limiting factor for them in that she does not feed them every time they cry for food. Through a multitude of such limiting experiences they learn to develop the capacity to differentiate themselves from others and from objects and to delay gratification. If there had been no limits, there would be no consciousness.

Our discussion so far may seem, at first glance, to be discouraging, but not when we probe more deeply. It is not by accident that the Hebrew myth that marks the beginning of human consciousness, Adam and Eve in the Garden of Eden, is portrayed in the context of a rebellion. Consciousness is born in the struggle against a limit, called there a prohibition. Going beyond the limit set by Yahweh is then punished by the acquiring of other limits which operate inwardly in the human being—anxiety, the feeling of alienation and guilt. But valuable qualities also come out of this experience of rebellion—the sense of personal responsibility and ultimately the possibility, born out of loneliness, of human love. Confronting limits for the human personality actually turns out to be *expansive*. *Limiting* and *expanding* thus go together.

Alfred Adler proposed that civilization arose out of our physical limitations, or what Adler called inferiority. Tooth for tooth and claw for claw, men and women were inferior to the wild animals. In the struggle against these limitations for their survival, human beings evolved their intelligence.

Heraclitus said, "Conflict is both king of all and father of all."[1] He was referring to the theme I am here stating: conflict presupposes limits, and the struggle with limits is actually the source of creative productions. The limits are as necessary as those provided by the banks of a river, without which the water would be dispersed on the earth and there would be no river—that is, the river is constituted by the tension between the flowing water and the banks. Art in the same way requires limits as a necessary factor in its birth.

Creativity arises out of the tension between spontaneity and limitations, the latter (like the river banks) forcing the spontaneity into the various forms which are essential to the work of art or poem. Again listen to Heraclitus: unwise people "do not understand how that which differs with itself is in agreement: harmony consists of opposing tension, like that of the bow and the lyre."[2] In a discussion of how he composed his music, Duke Ellington explained that since his trumpet player could reach certain notes beautifully but not other notes, and the same with his trombonist, he had to write his music within those limits. "It's good to have limits," he remarked.

True, in our age there is occurring a new valuation of spontaneity and a strong reaction against rigidity. This goes along with a rediscovery of the values of the childlike capacity to play. In modern art, as we all know, there has evolved a new interest in children's painting as well as in peasant and primitive art, and these kinds of spontaneity often are used as models for adult art work. This is especially true in psychotherapy. The great majority of patients experience themselves as stifled and inhibited by the excessive and rigid limits insisted on by their parents. One of their reasons for coming for therapy in the first place is this conviction that all of this needs to be thrown overboard. Even if it is simplistic, this urge toward spontaneity obviously should be valued by the therapist. People must recover the "lost" aspects of their personalities, lost under a pile of inhibitions, if they are to become integrated in any effective sense.

But we must not forget that these stages in therapy, like children's art, are interim stages. Children's art is characterized by an unfinished quality. Despite the apparent similarity with non-objective art, it still lacks the tension necessary for authentic mature art. It is a promise but not yet an achievement. Sooner or later the growing person's art must relate itself to the dialectic tension that comes out of confronting limits and is present in all forms of mature art. Michelangelo's writhing slaves; Van Gogh's fiercely twisting cypress trees; Cézanne's lovely yellow-green landscapes of southern France, reminding us of the freshness of eternal spring—these works have that spontaneity, but they also have the mature quality that comes from the absorption of tension. This makes them much more than "interesting"; it makes them great. The controlled and transcended tension present in the work of art is the result of the artists' successful struggle with and against limits.

2. FORM AS A LIMITATION
IN CREATIVITY

The significance of limits in art is seen most clearly when we consider the question of form.

Form provides the essential boundaries and structure for the creative act. It is no accident that the art critic Clive Bell, in his books about Cézanne, cites "significant form" as the key to understanding the great painter's work.

Let us say I draw a rabbit on a blackboard. You say, "There's a rabbit." In reality there is nothing at all on the blackboard except the simple line I have made: no protrusion, nothing three dimensional, no indentation. It is the same blackboard as it was, and there can be no rabbit "on" it. You see only my chalk line, which may be infinitesimally narrow. This line limits the content. It says what space is *within* the picture and what is *outside*—it is a pure limiting to that particular form. The rabbit appears because you have accepted my communication that this space within the line is that which I wish to demarcate.

There is in this limiting a nonmaterial character, a spiritual character if you will, that is necessary in all creativity. Hence, *form* and, similarly, *design, plan,* and *pattern* all refer to a nonmaterial meaning present in the limits.

Our discussion of form demonstrates something else—that the object you see is a product both of your subjectivity *and* external reality. The form is born out of a dialectical relation between my brain (which is subjective, *in* me) and the object that I see external to me (which is objective). As Immanuel Kant insisted, we not only know the world, but the world at the same time conforms to our ways of knowing. Incidentally, note the word *conform*—the world forms itself "with," it takes on our forms.

The trouble begins whenever anyone dogmatically sets himself or herself up to defend either extreme. On the one hand, when an individual insists on his or her own subjectivity and follows exclusively his or her own imagination, we have a person whose flights of fancy may be interesting but who never really relates to the objective world. When, on the other hand, an individual insists that there is nothing "there" except empirical reality, we have a technologically minded person who would impoverish and oversimplify his or her and our lives. Our perception is determined by our imagination as well as by the empirical facts of the outside world.

Speaking of poetry, Coleridge distinguished between two kinds of form. One is external to the poet—the mechanical form, let us say, of the sonnet. This consists of an arbitrary agreement that the sonnet will consist of fourteen lines in a certain pattern. The other kind of form is organic. This is inner form. It comes from the poet, and consists of the passion he or she puts into the poem. The organic aspect of form causes it to grow on its own; it speaks to us down through the ages revealing new meaning to each generation. Centuries later we may find meaning in it that even the author did not know was there.

When you write a poem, you discover that the very necessity of fitting your meaning into such and such a form requires you to search in your imagination for new meanings. You reject certain ways of saying it; you select others, always trying to form the poem again. In your forming, you arrive at new and more profound meanings than you had even dreamed of. Form is not a mere lopping off of meaning that you don't have room to put into your poem; it is an aid to finding new meaning, a stimulus to condensing your meaning, to simplifying and purifying it, and to discovering on a more universal dimension the essence you wish to express. How much meaning Shakespeare could put into his plays *because* they were written in blank verse rather than prose, or his sonnets *because* they were fourteen lines!

In our day the concept of form is often attacked because of its relation to "formality" and "formalism," both of which—so we are told—are to be avoided like the plague. I agree that in transitional times like our own, when honesty of style is difficult to come by, formalism and formality should be required to demonstrate their authenticity. But in the attack on these often bastardized kinds of formalism, it is not form itself that is being accused, but special kinds of form—generally the conformist, dead kinds, which actually do lack an inner, organic vitality.

We should remember, moreover, that all spontaneity carries with it its own form. Anything expressed in language, for example, carries the forms given to it by that language. How different a poem originally written in English sounds when translated into the exquisite music of the French language or into the profound and powerful sentiments of the German language! Another example is the rebellion in the name of spontaneity against picture frames, as shown in those paintings that reach out over their frames, dramatically breaking the latter's too limiting boundaries. This act borrows its spontaneous power from the assumption of a frame to start with.

The juxtaposition of spontaneity and form are, of course, present all through human history. It is the ancient but ever-modern struggle of the Dionysian versus the Apollonian. In transitional periods this dichotomy comes completely out in the open since old forms do have to be transcended. I can, therefore, understand the rebellion in our day against form and limits as expressed in the cry "We have unlimited potentialities." But when these movements try to throw form or limits out entirely, they become self-destructive and noncreative. Never is form itself superseded so long as creativity endures. If form were to vanish, spontaneity would vanish with it.

3. IMAGINATION AND FORM

Imagination is the outreaching of mind. It is the individual's capacity to accept the bombardment of the conscious mind with ideas, impulses, images, and every other sort of psychic phenomena welling up from the preconscious. It is the capacity to "dream dreams and see visions," to consider diverse possibilities, and to endure the tension involved in holding these possibilities before one's attention. Imagination is casting off mooring ropes, taking one's chances that there will be new mooring posts in the vastness ahead.

In creative endeavors the imagination operates in juxtaposition with form. When these endeavors are successful, it is because imagination infuses form with its own vitality. The question is: How far can we let our imagination loose? Can we give it rein? Dare to think the unthinkable? Dare to conceive of, and move among, new visions?

At such times we face the danger of losing our orientation, the danger of complete isolation. Will we lose our accepted language, which makes communication possible in a shared world? Will we lose the boundaries that enable us to orient ourselves to what we call reality? This, again, is the problem of form, or stated differently, the awareness of limits.

Psychologically speaking, this is experienced by many people as psychosis. Hence some psychotics walk close to the wall in hospitals. They keep oriented to the edges, always preserving their localization in the external environment. Having no localization inwardly, they find it especially important to retain whatever outward localization is available.

As director of a large mental hospital in Germany which received many brain-injured soldiers during the war, Dr. Kurt Goldstein found that these patients suffered radical limitation of their capacities for imagination. He observed that they had to keep their closets in rigid array, shoes always placed in just this position, shirts hung in just that place. Whenever a closet was upset, the patient became panicky. He could not orient himself to the new arrangement, could not imagine a new "form" that would bring order out of the chaos. The patient was then thrown into what Goldstein called the "catastrophic situation." Or when asked to write his name on a sheet of paper, the brain-injured person would write the name in some corner close to the boundaries. He could not tolerate the possibility of becoming lost in the open spaces. His capacities for abstract thought, for transcending the immediate facts in terms of the possible—what I call, in this context, imagination—were severely curtailed. He felt powerless to change the environment to make it adequate to his needs.

Such behavior is indicative of what life is when imaginative powers are cut off. The limits have always to be kept clear and visible. Lacking the ability to shift forms, these patients found their world radically truncated. Any "limitless" existence was experienced by them as being highly dangerous.

Not brain-injured, you and I nevertheless can experience a similar anxiety in the reverse situation—that is, in the creative act. The boundaries of our world shift under our feet and we tremble while waiting to see whether any new form will take the place of the lost boundary or whether we can create out of this chaos some new order.

As imagination gives vitality to form, form keeps imagination from driving us into psychosis. This is the ultimate necessity of limits. Artists are the ones who have the capacity to see original visions. They typically have powerful imaginations and, at the same time, a sufficiently developed sense of form to avoid being led into the catastrophic situation. They are the frontier scouts who go out ahead of the rest of us to explore the future. We can surely tolerate their special dependencies and harmless idiosyncracies. For we will be better prepared for the future if we can listen seriously to them.

There is a curiously sharp sense of joy—or perhaps better expressed, a sense of mild ecstasy—that comes when you find the particular form required by your creation. Let us say you have been puzzling about it for days when suddenly you get the insight that unlocks the door—you see how to write that line, what combination of colors is needed in your picture, how to form that theme you may be writing for a class, or you hit upon the theory to fit your new facts. I have often wondered about this special sense of joy; it so often seems out of proportion to what actually has happened.

I may have worked at my desk morning after morning trying to find a way to express some important idea. When my "insight" suddenly breaks through—which may happen when I am chopping wood in the afternoon—I experience a strange lightness in my step as though a great load were taken off my shoulders, a sense of joy on a deeper level that continues without any relation whatever to the mundane tasks that I may be performing at the time. It cannot be just that the problem at hand has been answered—that generally brings only a sense of relief. What is the source of this curious pleasure?

I propose that it is the experience of this-is-the-way-things-are-meant-to-be. If only for that moment, we participate in the myth of creation. Order comes out of disorder, form out of chaos, as it did in the creation of the universe. The sense of joy comes from our participation, no matter how slight, in being as such. The paradox is that at that moment we also experience more vividly our own limitations. We discover the *amor fati* that Nietzsche writes about—the love of one's fate. No wonder it gives a sense of ecstasy!

SEVEN

◻

PASSION FOR FORM

FOR MANY YEARS I have been convinced that something occurs in the creative working of the imagination that is more fundamental—but more puzzling—than we have assumed in contemporary psychology. In our day of dedication to facts and hard-headed objectivity, we have disparaged imagination: it gets us away from "reality"; it taints our work with "subjectivity"; and, worst of all, it is said to be unscientific. As a result, art and imagination are often taken as the "frosting" to life rather than as the solid food. No wonder people think of "art" in terms of its cognate, "artificial," or even consider it a luxury that slyly fools us, "artifice." Throughout Western history our dilemma has been whether imagination shall turn out to be artifice or the source of being.

What if imagination and art are not frosting at all, but the fountainhead of human experience? What if our logic and science derive from art forms and are fundamentally dependent on them rather than art being merely a decoration for our work when science and logic have produced it? These are the hypotheses I propose here.

This same problem is related to psychotherapy in ways that are much more profound than merely the play on words. In other words, is psychotherapy an artifice, a process that is characterized by artificiality, or is it a process that can give birth to new being?

1

Pondering these hypotheses, I brought data to my aid from the dreams of persons in therapy. By dreaming, persons in analysis, I saw, are doing something on a level quite below that of psychodynamics. They are struggling with their world —to make sense out of nonsense, meaning out of chaos, coherence out of conflict. They are doing it by imagination, by constructing new forms and relationships in their world, and by achieving through proportion and perspective a world in which they can survive and live with some meaning.

Here is a simple dream. It was related by an intelligent man who seems younger than his thirty years, coming from a culture where fathers have considerable authority.

I was in the sea playing with some large porpoises. I like porpoises and wanted these to be like pets. Then I began to get afraid, thinking that the big porpoises would hurt me. I went out of the water, on the shore, and now I seem to be a cat hanging by its tail from a tree. The cat is curled up in a teardrop form, but its eyes are big and seductive, one of them winking. A porpoise comes up, and like a father cajoling a youngster out of bed with "get up and get going," it hits the cat lightly. The cat then becomes afraid with a real panic and bounds off in a straight line into the higher rocks, away from the sea.

Let us put aside such obvious symbols as the big porpoises being father and so on—symbols that are almost always confused with symptoms. I ask you to take the dream as an abstract painting, to look at it as pure form and motion.

We see first a smallish form, namely the boy, playing with the larger forms, the porpoises. Imagine the former as a small circle, and the latter as large circles. The playing movement conveys a kind of love in the dream, which we could express by lines toward each other converging in the play. In the second scene we see the smaller form (the boy in his fright) moving in a line out of the sea and away from the larger forms. The third scene shows the smaller form as a cat, now in an elliptical, tearlike, form, the coyness of the cat's eyes being seductive. The big form now coming toward the cat moves into the cajoling act and the lines here, it seems to me, would be confused. This is a typical neurotic phase consisting of the dreamer trying to resolve his relationship with his father and the world. And, of course, it does not work. The fourth and last scene is the panic in which the smaller form, the cat, moves rapidly out of the scene. It dashes toward the higher rocks. The motion is in a straight line off the canvas. The whole dream can be seen as an endeavor through form and motion to resolve this young man's relationship, in its love and its fear, to his father and father figures.

The resolution is a vivid failure. But the "painting" or play, Ionescolike though it be, shows like many a contemporary drama the vital tension in the irresolution of conflict. Therapeutically speaking, the patient is certainly facing his conflicts, albeit he can at the moment do nothing but flee.

We also can see in these scenes a progression of planes: first, the plane of the sea; second, the higher plane of the land with the tree; and third, the highest plane of all, namely the rocks on the mountain to which the cat leaps. These may be conceived as higher levels of consciousness to which the dreamer climbs. This expansion of consciousness may represent an important gain for the patient even though in the dream the actual resolution of the problem is a failure.

When we turn such a dream into an abstract painting, we are on a deeper level than psychodynamics. I do not mean we should leave out the contents of the dreams of our patients. I mean we should go beyond contents to the ground forms. We shall then be dealing with basic *forms* that only later, and derivatively, become *formulations*.

From the most obvious viewpoint, the son is trying to work out a better relationship with his father, to be accepted as a comrade, let us say. But on a deeper level he is trying to construct a world that makes sense, that has space and motion and keeps these in some proportion, a world that he can live in. *You can live without a father who accepts you, but you cannot live without a world that makes some sense to you.* Symbol in this sense no longer means symptom. As I have pointed out elsewhere,[1] *symbol* returns to its original and root meaning of "drawing together" (*sym-ballein*). The problem—the neurosis and its elements—is described by the antonym of *symbolic*, namely *diabolic* (*dia-ballein*), "pulling apart."

Dreams are *par excellence* the realm of symbols and myths. I use the term *myth* not in the pejorative sense of "falsehood," but in the sense of *a form of universal truth* revealed in some partial way to the dreamer. These are ways human consciousness makes sense of the world. Persons in therapy, like all of us, are trying to make sense out of nonsense, trying to put the world into some perspective, trying to form out of the chaos they are suffering some order and harmony.

After having studied a series of dreams of persons in therapy, I am convinced that there is one quality that is always present, a quality I call *passion for form*. The patient constructs in his "unconscious" a drama; it has a beginning, something happens and is "flashed on the stage," and then it comes to some kind of denouement. I have noted the forms in the dreams being repeated, revised, remolded, and then, like a motif in a symphony, returning triumphantly to be drawn together to make a meaningful whole of the series.

2

I found that one fruitful approach is *to take the dream as a series of spatial forms*. I refer now to a thirty-year-old woman in therapy. In one stage in her dreams, a female character, for example, would move onto the stage of the dream; then another female would enter; a male would appear; the females would exit together. This kind of movement in space occurred in the Lesbian period of this particular person's analysis. In later dreams she, the patient, would enter; then the female, who was present, would exit; a man would enter and he would sit beside her. I began to see a curious geometric communication, a progression of spatial forms. Perhaps the meaning of her dreams, and the progress of her analysis, could be better understood by how she constructed these forms moving in space—of which she was quite unaware—than in what she verbalized about her dreams.

Then I began to notice the presence of triangles in this person's dreams. First, in her dreams referring to her infantile period, it was the triangle of father, mother, and baby. In what I took to be her adolescent phase, the triangle was composed of two women and a man, and she, as one of the women, moved in space toward the man. Then after some months of analysis, in a Lesbian phase, the triangle consisted of two women and a man with the two women standing together. In a still later period the triangles turned into rectangles: two men were in the dream with two women, assumedly her boy friend, herself, her mother, and her father. Her development then became a process of working through rectangles to form eventually a new triangle, her man, herself, and a child. These dreams occurred in the middle and later parts of the analysis.

That the symbol of the triangle is fundamental can be seen by the fact that it refers to a number of different levels simultaneously. A triangle has three lines; it has the lowest possible number of straight lines required to make a geometric form that has content. This is the mathematical, "pure form" level. The triangle is fundamental in early, neolithic art—*vide* designs on the vases of this period. This is the aesthetic level. It is present in science—triangulation is the way the Egyptians figured their relation to the stars. The triangle is the basic symbol in medieval philosophy and theology—*vide* the Trinity. It is fundamental in Gothic art, a graphic example of which is Mont-Saint-Michel, the triangle of rock rising from the sea capped by the Gothic triangle of man-built architecture which, in turn, ends in a pinnacle pointing toward heaven—a magnificent art form in which we have the triangle of nature, man, and God. And finally, psychologically speaking, we have the basic human triangle—man, woman, and child.

The importance of forms is revealed in the inescapable unity of the body with the world. The body is always a part of the world. I sit on this chair; the chair is on a floor in this building; and the building, in turn, rests on the mountain of stone that is Manhattan Island. Whenever I walk, my body is interrelated with the world in which and on which I take my steps. This presupposes some harmony between body and world. We know from physics that the earth rises infinitesimally to meet my step, as any two bodies attract each other. The *balance* essential in walking is one that is not solely in my body; it can be understood only as a relationship of my body to the ground on which it stands and walks. The earth is there to meet each foot as it falls, and the rhythm of my walking depends on my faith that the earth will be there.

Our active need for form is shown in the fact that we automatically construct it in an infinite number of ways. The mime Marcel Marceau stands upon the stage impersonating a man taking his dog out for a walk. Marceau's arm is outstretched as though holding the dog's leash. As his arm jerks back and forth, everyone in the audience "sees" the dog straining at the leash to sniff this or that in the bushes. Indeed, the dog and the leash are the most "real" parts of the scene even though there is no dog and no leash on the stage at all. Only part of the Gestalt is there—the man Marceau and his arm. The rest is entirely supplied by our imagination as viewers. The incomplete Gestalt is completed in our fantasy. Another mime, Jean-Louis Barrault, who plays a deaf-mute in the film *Les Enfants du Paradis*, goes through the whole account of the man who has had his pocket picked in the crowd —he makes one movement for the fat stomach of the victim, another movement for the dour expression of the companion, and so on until we have a vivid picture of the entire event of the pickpocketing. But not a word has been spoken. There is only a mime making a few artful motions. All of the gaps are automatically filled by our imagination.

The human imagination leaps to form the whole, to complete the scene in order to make sense of it. The instantaneous way this is done shows how we are driven to construct the remainder of the scene. To fill the gaps is essential if the scene is to have meaning. That we may do this in misleading ways—at times in neurotic or paranoid ways—does not gainsay the central point. Our passion for form expresses our yearning to make the world adequate to our needs and desires, and, more important, to experience ourselves as having significance.

The phrase "passion for form," may be interesting, but it is also problematical. If we used just the word *form*, it would sound too abstract; but when it is combined with passion, we see that what is meant is not form in any intellectual sense, but rather in a wholistic scene. What is occurring in the person, hidden as it may be by passivity or other neurotic symptoms, is a conflict-filled passion to make sense out of a crisis-ridden life.

Plato told us long ago how passion, or, as he

put it, Eros, moves toward the creation of form. Eros moves toward the making of meaning and the revealing of Being. Originally a daimon called love, Eros is the lover of wisdom, and the force in us that brings to birth both wisdom and beauty. Plato says through Socrates that "human nature will not easily find a helper better than love [Eros]."[2] "All creation or passage of non-being into being is poetry or making," Plato writes, "and the processes of all art are creative; and the masters of arts are all poets or makers."[3] Through Eros or the passion of love, which is daimonic and constructive at the same time, Plato looks forward to "at last the vision . . . of a single science, which is the science of beauty everywhere."[4]

Thus the mathematicians and physicists talk about the "elegance" of a theory. Utility is subsumed as part of the character of being beautiful. The harmony of an internal form, the inner consistency of a theory, the character of beauty that touches your sensibilities—these are significant factors that determine why one given insight comes into consciousness rather than another. As a psychoanalyst, I can only add that my experience in helping people achieve insights from unconscious dimensions within themselves reveals the same phenomenon—insights emerge not chiefly because they are "intellectually true" or even because they are helpful, but because they have a certain *form*, the form that is beautiful because it completes what is incomplete in us.

This idea, this new form that suddenly presents itself, comes in order to complete a hitherto incomplete Gestalt with which we are struggling in conscious awareness. One can quite accurately speak of this unfinished pattern, this unformed form, as constituting the "call" to which our preconscious, out of its maelstrom, gives an answer.

4

By passion for form I mean a principle of human experience that is analogous to several of the most important ideas in Western history. Kant proposed that our understanding is not simply a reflection of the objective world around us, but it also *constitutes* this world. It is not that objects simply speak to *us*; they also conform to our ways of knowing. The mind thus is an active process of forming and re-forming the world.

Interpreting dreams as dramas of the patient's relationship to his or her world, I asked myself whether there is not on a deeper and more inclusive level in human experience something parallel to what Kant was talking about. That is, is it not only our *intellectual* understanding that plays a role in our forming and re-forming the world in the process of knowing it, but do not *imagination* and *emotions* also play a critical role? It must be the *totality* of ourselves that understands, not simply reason. And it is the totality of ourselves that fashions the images to which the world conforms.

Not only does reason form and re-form the world, but the "preconscious," with its impulses and needs, does so also and does so on the basis of wish and intentionality. Human beings not only think but feel and will as they make form in their world. This is why I use the word *passion*, the sum of erotic and dynamic tendencies, in the phrase "passion for form." Persons in therapy—or anybody for that matter—are not simply engaged in knowing their world: what they are engaged in is a passionate re-forming of their world by virtue of their interrelationship with it.

This passion for form is a way of trying to find and constitute meaning in life. And this is what genuine creativity is. Imagination, broadly defined, seems to me to be a principle in human life underlying even reason, for the rational functions, according to our definitions, can lead to understanding—can participate in the constituting of reality—only as they are creative. Creativity is thus involved in our every experience as we try to make meaning in our self-world relationship.

Philosopher Alfred North Whitehead also

speaks in effect of this passion for form. Whitehead has constructed a philosophy based not on reason alone, but one that includes what he calls "feeling." By feeling he does not mean simply affect. As I understand it he means the total capacity of the human organism to experience his or her world. Whitehead reformulates Descartes' original principle as follows:

Descartes was wrong when he said "Cogito, ergo sum"—I think, therefore I am. It is never bare thought or bare existence that we are aware of. I find myself rather as essentially a unity of emotions, of enjoyment, of hopes, of fears, of regrets, valuations of alternatives, decisions—all of these are subjective reactions to my environment as I am active in my nature. My unity which is Descartes' "I am" is my *process of shaping this welter of material into a consistent pattern of feelings.*[5]

What I am calling passion for form is, if I understand Whitehead aright, a central aspect of what he is describing as the experience of identity.* I am able to shape feelings, sensibilities, enjoyments, hopes into a pattern that makes me

---

* A friend of mine, on reading this chapter in manuscript, sent me the following original poem, which I quote with permission:

> I am, therefore I love
> the total sensibility
> that looked at me
> out of your undefended face
> immediately.
> I love, therefore I am.

aware of myself as man or woman. But I cannot shape them into a pattern as a purely subjective act. I can do it only as I am related to the immediate objective world in which I live.

Passion can destroy the self. But this is not passion for form; it is passion gone beserk. Passion obviously can be diabolic as well as symbolic —it can deform as well as form; it can destroy meaning and produce chaos again. When sexual powers emerge in puberty, passion often does destroy form temporarily. But sex also has great creative potentialities precisely because it is passion. Unless one's development is radically pathological, there will also occur in the adolescent a growth toward a new form, in manhood or womanhood, in contrast to his or her previous state as girl or boy.

5

The urgent need in everyone to give form to his or her life can be illustrated by the case of a young man who consulted with me when I was writing this chapter. He was the only son in a professional family where his mother and father had quarreled and had fought almost continuously, according to his memory, since he was born. He had never been able to concentrate or apply himself to his studies in school. As a boy when he was supposed to be studying in his room, he would hear his father coming up the stairs and immediately open a schoolbook to cover over the magazine on mechanics he had been looking at. He recalled that his father, a successful but apparently very cold man, had often promised to take him on various trips as a reward if he successfully got through his schoolwork. But none of those trips ever materialized.

His mother had made him her confidante, covertly supporting him in his conflicts with his father. He and his mother used to sit out in the backyard summer evenings talking until late at night—they were "partners," they "grooved together," as he put it. His father exercised pull to get him accepted into college in another part of the country; but the young man spent three months there never going out of his room until his father came to fetch him home.

Living at home he worked as a carpenter, and later as a construction worker in the Peace Corps. He then came to New York where he supported himself as a plumber, doing sculpture on the side, until by a kind of lucky accident he got a job as instructor in crafts at a university an hour outside the city. But in his job he was unable to assert himself or to talk clearly and directly to either students or faculty. He was overawed by the young Ivy League graduates on the faculty who monopolized faculty meetings with their chatter which he felt was pompous and artificial. In this dazed and ineffectual state, he first began work with me. I found him an unusually sensitive person, generous, talented (he gave me a wire sculptured figure he had made in my waiting room which I found delightful). He was seriously withdrawn and apparently accomplishing practically nothing in his job or life.

We worked together a couple of times a week for most of a year, in which time he made unusually commendable progress in his interpersonal relationships. He now worked effectually and had entirely overcome his neurotic awe of fellow faculty members. He and I agreed that since he was now functioning actively and well we would stop our work for the time being. We were both aware, however, that we had never been able to explore adequately his relationship with his mother.

He came back a year later. He had married in the meantime, but this did not seem to present any special problems. What cued off the present impasse was a visit he and his wife had made the previous month to his mother, who by that time was in a mental hospital. They found her sitting by the nurses' desk in the corridor "waiting for her cigarette." She went into her room to talk with them, but soon came out again to continue waiting out the hour until the time for her rationed cigarette.

Coming back on the train, the young man was very depressed. He had known theoretically about his mother's increasingly senile condition, but was unable to make emotional sense of it. His withdrawn, apathetic state was similar to but also different from his condition the first time he had come. He was now able to communicate with me directly and openly. His problem was localized, specific, in contrast to the generalized daze he had been suffering from the first time he came. His relationship to his mother was in chaos. In that segment of his life he felt no form at all, only a gnawing confusion.

After our first session the daze he was under lifted, but the problem remained. This is often the function of *communication* in the therapeutic hour: it enables the person to overcome his or her sense of alienation from the human kind. But it does not suffice in itself for a genuine experience of new form. It assuages, but it doesn't produce the new form. An overcoming of the chaos on a deeper level is required, and this can only be done with some kind of insight.

In this second hour we reviewed at length his mother's attachment to him and the understandable upset he would feel at her present condition, even though he had known it had been coming on for years. She had privately made him the "crown prince." I pointed out that she had been a powerful woman in these fights with his father, that she had wooed him away from his father and had exploited him in her endeavors to defeat his father. In contrast to his illusion that they had been partners or that they had "grooved," he actually had been a hostage, a little person used in much bigger battles. When he mentioned his surprise at seeing these things, he brought to my mind a story, which I told him. A man was selling hamburgers allegedly made of rabbit meat at an amazingly low price. When people asked him how he did it, he admitted that he was using some horse meat. But when this did not suffice as an explanation, he confessed it was 50 per cent horse meat and 50 per cent rabbit meat. When they continued to ask him what he meant, he stated, "One rabbit to one horse."

The graphic image of the rabbit and horse gave him a powerful "aha" experience, much greater than any he would have gotten from an intellectual explanation. He continued to marvel at his being the rabbit not in any derogatory sense, but with the felt realization of how helpless he must have been in his childhood. A heavy load of guilt and previously unexpressed hostility was lifted off his back. The image gave him a way of getting at long last to his negative feelings toward his mother. Many details of his background now fell into place, and he seemed to be able to cut the psychological umbilical cord which he previously did not know existed.

Curiously, persons in such situations give the impression of having had all along the necessary strength at hand to make these changes; it was just a matter of waiting for the "sun of order" to melt away "the fog of confusion" (to change the metaphor into Delphic-oracle terms). The "passion" in his example is shown by the alacrity with which he grasped this insight and by the immediacy with which he re-formed his psychological world. He gave the impression—which again is typical for the experience—of having stored up the strength at previous stages until it was finally possible, on getting the right piece of the jigsaw puzzle, to suddenly seize that strength and exercise it.

In our third and last session he told me of his newly-made decision to resign his post at the university, and to find a studio in which he could devote himself entirely to his sculpture.

The communication with me in the first session may be seen as the preliminary step in this creative process. Then came the "aha" experience as the needed insight, preferably as an image, is born in the individual's consciousness. The third step is the making of the decisions, which the young man did between the second and third sessions, as *a result* of the newly achieved form. The therapist cannot predict the exact nature of such decisions; they are *a living out of the new form.*

The creative process is the expression of this passion for form. It is the struggle against disintegration, the struggle to bring into existence new kinds of being that give harmony and integration.

Plato has for our summation some charming advice:

For he who would proceed aright in this manner should begin in youth to visit beautiful forms; and first, if he be guided by his instructor aright, to love one such form only—out of that he should create fair thoughts; and soon he will of himself perceive that the beauty of one form is akin to the beauty of another, and that beauty in every form is one and the same.[6]

NOTES

TWO The Nature of Creativity, pp. 33–56

1. Ludwig Binswanger, in *Existence: A New Dimension in Psychology and Psychiatry*, eds. Rollo May, Ernest Angel, and Henri F. Ellenberger (New York, 1958), p. 11.

THREE Creativity and the Unconscious, pp. 57–85

1. This was in the mid-1940s, when being pregnant and unwed was considerably more traumatic than now.

2. Henri Poincaré, "Mathematical Creation," from *The Foundation of Science*, trans. George Bruce Halsted, in *The Creative Process*, ed. Brewester Ghiselin (New York, 1952), p. 36.

3. *Ibid.*, p. 37.

4. *Ibid.*, p. 38.

5. *Ibid.*

6. *Ibid.*

7. *Ibid.*, p. 40.

8. Werner-Heisenberg, "The Representation of Nature in Contemporary Physics," in *Symbolism in Religion and Literature*, ed. Rollo May (New York, 1960), p. 225.

9. Yevgeny Yevtushenko, *The Poetry of Yevgeny Yevtushenko, 1953–1965*, trans. George Reavey (New York, 1965), pp. x–xi. Emphasis mine.

10. *Ibid.*, p. vii.
11. *Ibid.*, p. viii–ix.

FOUR Creativity and Encounter, pp. 87–109

1. Archibald MacLeish, *Poetry and Experience* (Boston, 1961), pp. 8–9.
2. *Ibid.*
3. James Lord, *A Giacometti Portrait* (New York, 1964), p. 26.
4. *Ibid.*, p. 22.
5. *Ibid.*, p. 23.
6. *Ibid.*, p. 18.
7. *Ibid.*, p. 24.
8. *Ibid.*, p. 41 (italics mine).
9. *Ibid.*, p. 38 (italics mine).
10. MacLeish, pp. 8–9.
11. Frank Barron, "Creation and Encounter," *Scientific American* (September, 1958), 1–9.

FIVE The Delphic Oracle as Therapist, pp. 111–131

1. E. R. Dodds, *The Greeks and the Irrational* (Berkeley, 1964), p. 75.
2. The word *tyrannos* refers simply to an absolute ruler, of the type normally spawned in eras of political ferment and change. Some of these "tyrants," like Pisistratus, the "tyrant of Athens" of the late sixth century, are regarded as benefactors by historians as well as by modern Greeks. I well recall my surprise when I first heard the boys of the school in Greece in which I taught speak of Pisistratus with the same quality of admiration, if not the same quantity, as people in this country speak of George Washington.
3. *Translations from the Poetry of Rainer Maria Rilke*, trans. M. D. Herter Norton (New York, 1938), p. 181.
4. Robert Flacelière, *Greek Oracles*, trans. Douglas Garman (New York, 1965), p. 49.
5. Dodds, p. 73.
6. *Ibid.*
7. Flacelière, p. 37.
8. Flacelière, p. 52.
9. Herodotus, *The Histories*, Book VII, 140–144.

SIX   On the Limits of Creativity, pp. 133–148

1. Heraclitus, p. 28, Ancilla to the Pre-Socratic Philosophers, A complete translation of the Fragments in Diels, by Kathleen Freeman, Harvard U. Press, Cambridge, Mass., 1970.

2. *Ibid.*, p. 28.

SEVEN   Passion for Form, pp. 149–169

1. Rollo May, "The Meaning of Symbols," in *Symbolism in Religion and Literature*, ed. Rollo May (New York, 1960), pp. 11–50.

2. Plato, *Symposium*, trans. Benjamin Jowett, in *The Portable Greek Reader*, ed. W. H. Auden (New York, 1948), p. 499.

3. *Ibid.*, p. 497.

4. Elsewhere in this book I have noted that the mathematician Poincaré echoes a similar emphasis on Eros as bringing forth both beauty and truth at once. (See p. 73.)

5. *Alfred North Whitehead: His Reflections on Man and Nature*, selected by Ruth Nanda Anshen (New York, 1961), p. 28. Emphasis mine.

6. Plato, p. 496.

ABOUT THE AUTHOR

DR. MAY has been a training and supervisory analyst at the William Alanson White Institute of Psychiatry, Psychoanalysis, and Psychology. He has taught at Harvard, Princeton and Yale and has been Regents' Professor at the University of California at Santa Cruz. He lectures extensively at universities and colleges. Reviewers and readers have been unanimous in the praise of the scholarly and pioneering contributions of Dr. May, outstanding among which are *The Meaning of Anxiety, Man's Search for Himself,* and the national bestseller *Love and Will,* which won the Ralph Waldo Emerson Award, given by Phi Beta Kappa.

Bantam
On Psychology

☐	23874	**HOW TO BREAK YOUR ADDICTION TO A PERSON** Howard M. Halpern, Ph.D.	$3.95
☐	01419	**IF YOU COULD HEAR WHAT I CANNOT SAY . . .** Nathaniel Branden (A Large Format Book)	$8.95
☐	23043	**ACTIVE LOVING** Ari Kiev, M.D.	$2.95
☐	22576	**PATHFINDERS** Gail Sheehy	$4.50
☐	24754	**PASSAGES: PREDICTABLE CRISES OF ADULT LIFE** Gail Sheehy	$4.95
☐	24966	**THE FAMILY CRUCIBLE** Dr. Napier	$4.95
☐	23399	**THE POWER OF YOUR SUBCONSCIOUS MIND** Dr. J. Murphy	$3.95
☐	23125	**FOCUSING** E. Grendlin	$3.95
☐	24518	**LOVE IS LETTING GO OF FEAR** Gerald Jampolsky	$3.50
☐	23818	**PEACE FROM NERVOUS SUFFERING** Claire Weekes	$3.95
☐	20540	**THE GESTALT APPROACH & EYE WITNESS TO THERAPY** Fritz Perls	$3.50
☐	24064	**THE BOOK OF HOPE** DeRosis & Pellegrino	$4.50
☐	23449	**THE PSYCHOLOGY OF SELF-ESTEEM: A New Concept of Man's Psychological Nature** Nathaniel Branden	$3.95
☐	23267	**WHAT DO YOU SAY AFTER YOU SAY HELLO?** Eric Berne, M.D.	$3.95
☐	20774	**GESTALT THERAPY VERBATIM** Fritz Perls	$3.50
☐	24038	**PSYCHO-CYBERNETICS AND SELF-FULFILLMENT** Maxwell Maltz, M.D.	$3.95
☐	24557	**THE DISOWNED SELF** Nathaniel Branden	$3.95
☐	24411	**CUTTING LOOSE: An Adult Guide for Coming To Terms With Your Parents** Howard Halpern	$3.95
☐	20977	**WHEN I SAY NO, I FEEL GUILTY** Manuel Smith	$3.95

Prices and availability subject to change without notice.

Buy them at your local bookstore or use this handy coupon for ordering:

Bantam Books, Inc., Dept. ME, 414 East Golf Road, Des Plaines, Ill. 60016

Please send me the books I have checked above. I am enclosing $_____
(please add $1.25 to cover postage and handling). Send check or money order
—no cash or C.O.D.'s please.

Mr/Mrs/Miss _____

Address _____

City _____ State/Zip _____

ME—12/84

Please allow four to six weeks for delivery. This offer expires 6/85.

We Deliver!
And So Do These Bestsellers.

SPECIAL
MONEY SAVING
OFFER

Now you can have an up-to-date listing of
Bantam's hundreds of titles plus take advantage
of our unique and exciting bonus book offer. A
special offer which gives you the opportunity to
purchase a Bantam book for only 50¢. Here's
how!

By ordering any five books at the regular price
per order, you can also choose any other single
book listed (up to a $4.95 value) for just 50¢.
Some restrictions do apply, but for further details why not send for Bantam's listing of titles
today!

Just send us your name and address plus 50¢
to defray the postage and handling costs.

BANTAM BOOKS, INC.
Dept. FC, 414 East Golf Road, Des Plaines, Ill 60016

Mr./Mrs./Miss/Ms. _____
　　　　　　　　　　　(please print)

Address _____

City_____ State_____ Zip_____
　　　　　　　　　　　　　　　　　　　　FC—3/84